Puerto Vallarta
& Acapulco

Berlitz Publishing Company, Inc.

Princeton   Mexico City   Dublin   Eschborn   Singapore

Berlitz Trademark Reg. U.S. Patent Office and other countries
Marca Registrada

Text:	Lynne Bairstow
Editor:	Alice Fellows
Photography:	Chris Coe except page 53 by Claude Huber
Cover Photo:	Chris Coe
Photo Editor:	Naomi Zinn
Layout:	Media Content Marketing, Inc.
Cartography:	Ortelius Design

The author would like to thank Claudia Velo for her help with research, fact checking, and manuscript preparation.

Although the publisher tries to insure the accuracy of all the information in this book, changes are inevitable and errors may result. The publisher cannot be responsible for any resulting loss, inconvenience, or injury. If you find an error in this guide, please let the editors know by writing to Berlitz Publishing Company, 400 Alexander Park, Princeton, NJ 08540-6306.

ISBN 2-8315-6984-2

Printed in Italy
010/010 NEW

CONTENTS

● A ☛ in the text denotes a highly recommended sight

Puerto Vallarta
& Acapulco

THE LAND AND ITS PEOPLE

The idyllic geography of Mexico's Pacific Coast has been both its calling card and its protector. For years, the countless coves and inlets along Mexico's western shore were closed off to the rest of the world, isolated by the jungle-studded mountains of the Sierra Madre Occidental. However, the deep azure waters and sheltered palm-fringed bays were simply too tempting to leave alone. From Spanish explorers to contemporary travelers, the lure of Pacific Mexico retains its natural beauty.

Alongside the brilliant blues of the water and the greens of the tropical jungles, you'll notice that the Mexican people are captivated by other bright colors—from vivid yellows and oranges to the vibrant *Rosa Mexicano* (hot pink). Even architectural styles incorporate these strong colors. All along the Costa Careyes, the elegant, open brilliantly colored villas have evolved as a type of architectural style, based on the work of Legorreta and Barragán. Even the small hillside houses overlooking downtown Manzanillo are colored in every imaginable hue, giving the impression of a mountainside mosaic.

If warm, brilliant colors are common along this coast, they are a reflection of the spirit of the people here. There's a genuine friendliness inherent in the residents of this coast. Yet, though Mexicans are bound together by their history and geography, Mexico has immense regional differences as marked as the variety of regional flavors in the food or the rhythms of the music. This becomes even more evident in coastal resort areas where an important percentage of the communities are people who have migrated here in search of the better standard of living—provided by the "almighty dollar," brought into the country by "amigos," also known as "turistas."

As these resorts along the Pacific Coast are places that have, for the most part, evolved from indigenous coastal communities, it helps to understand something of the people who live there, and of their culture.

Jalisco, Puerto Vallarta's home state, is a land of proud, hardworking people. They receive tourists with an accepting smile, treating them as friends, and offering their most sincere hospitality. In Jalisco a man's word is still his most valued possession, and traditional family values and structures are still very much alive. In the smaller towns the women still walk to the earliest mass, and marriages are arranged between families.

As you progress south along the coast the lack of settlements will underscore the difficulties imposed by this region's dramatic geography. Nevertheless, for centuries the people of these coastal communities have been content to live by fishing, growing a few crops, raising a few animals, and enjoying a simple life surrounded by the most basic of comforts and the warmth of both their families and the weather. In recent years, well-to-do foreigners found this to be an ideal retreat, meeting their desire for both seclusion and exclusivity as well as being a place that seems to be designed by nature for the most discriminating of tastes. The locals welcomed them, respecting their frequently extravagant tastes and occasionally scandalous behavior—in such sharp contrast to the simple and quiet lives they themselves had led.

Along the Costa Alegre, you may find the people who work there are so efficient as to become almost invisible— their only purpose in mind seems to be to please the *patrón*. This is an inherent attitude—the people of this area take pride in a job well done. This attitude may be a little disturbing for visitors coming from places where hired help is

In Puerto Vallarta and Acapulco, visitors quickly discover why everyone loves to smile—they'll have you smiling too!

somewhat of a luxury or even an aberration, but in Mexico, it is just a way of life.

Yet don't mistake service for submission—it is not meant to encourage a patronizing attitude on the part of the visitor. Mexicans everywhere are proud of what they do and who they are. They should not to be considered uneducated just because they see life in a different manner, and they are not "poor" just because they don't live in an air-conditioned, cable-ready house. Nor are they always looking for a tip—sometimes a sincere smile is more appreciated.

The people in the state of **Colima,** home state of the southern end of the Costa Alegre and Manzanillo, seem to have as mild a temperament as the land itself. Here, the mountains appear to roll into the sea, and the fertile valleys extend into the horizon. For whatever reason, the people here were known as far back as Aztec times for their quiet and peaceful spirit.

The state of **Guerrero** is a more exotic land. In Guerrero, where Acapulco and Zihuatanejo are located, the heat is evident not only in the weather but also in the people. Women seem to sway their hips as naturally as the waves rolling into shore, and men are quick-tempered, always ready to prove their point in a very physical manner.

The people of **Oaxaca** tend to be quiet and mysterious, and sometimes may appear to be distant. A people with a long past, they seem to prefer to sit quietly and see what the newcomers bring into their lands and their lives before passing judgment.

Characteristic of all these communities is the striking contrasts that are apparent everywhere. In Puerto Vallarta, it may be the glimpse of a burro loaded down with palm branches clopping alongside a taxi; in Acapulco it may be a businessman dressed in a suit standing in line at the bank alongside a Zapotec Indian woman in a brightly embroidered *huipil* (blouse), or the contrast between a palapa restaurant on Playa La Ropa with the elegant cliffside dining in Ixtapa.

Along the Pacific Coast

Each beach resort and town along the coast has its own particular appeal, and being more familiar with them can help you in selecting the area that will best meet your expectations.

Puerto Vallarta's appeal sneaks up on you with its succession of picturesque everyday scenes: the sight of laughing children being photographed on one of the waterfront public sculptures, or a glimpse of brilliant bougainvillea spilling over a balcony up a side street. No matter what it is that draws you in, no other place in Mexico so perfectly combines the gentle feeling of a traditional *pueblo* with the convenience and comforts of a sophisticated resort.

Traveling south along the coast is an area of unparalleled beaches, a 145-mile stretch of road that connects tropical forests with dramatic cliff-lined coves, known as the **Costa Alegre.** It's mostly an area of exclusive, privileged resorts, but also offers a few funky beachfront places to stay. You come here for privacy, seclusion, and immersion in nature.

Manzanillo, at the southern end of the Costa Alegre, has been around a long time; its harbor was used for shipbuilding and Pacific trade in the 16th century. The town of Manzanillo itself is traditional and tranquil, and its offshore waters are noted for their exceptional sportfishing, as well as for the delicious fresh shrimp and fish brought in from the working port.

Zihuatanejo, a tiny fishing village between Manzanillo and Acapulco, attracts offbeat travelers with its sparkling bay and pristine, secluded beaches. FONATUR, the government agency that created Cancún, selected the area to develop the planned community of **Ixtapa.** Today the pair make an inviting duo: Zihuatanejo for the charm of a village and Ixtapa for its manicured luxury.

After sunset, the lights in Puerto Vallarta burn bright —a beacon for a fiesta.

For years, **Acapulco** was Mexico's principal attraction for international travelers. Acapulco was the kind of place for which the phrase "jet set" was invented, the winter playground of the pampered. The first view of Acapulco coming in from the airport, is a sweeping bay with white ships on blue water, a long curving beach lined with high-rise hotels, and the city cradled in the arm of green hills. It looks like a large, rather unkempt city, almost incongruous as a beach resort. However at night, after the sun sets and the lights begin to sparkle, you understand why it still holds such an allure to travelers—the view of the bay at night and the vibrancy of its famed nightlife are simply seductive.

The Pacific Coast that borders Oaxaca state has become known as the area to choose if what you are looking for are pristine, wild, unspoiled beaches. The first to gain recognition was **Puerto Escondido,** considered one of the world's top surfing sites. Throughout the year, the town attracts a young and very hip international crowd, with its laid-back village ambiance, attractive and value-priced accommodations, and nearby nature excursions.

The planned development of the **Bays of Huatulco** is another project of FONATUR, with its 35 km (22 miles) of spectacular coastline spread across nine bays. Huatulco has evolved slowly, and those who travel here have the opportunity to enjoy an unparalleled combination of virgin beaches, modern facilities, and delicious tranquility.

The grandest of the sheltered bays that once appealed to conquistadors and pirates are the same ones that attract those in search of relaxation and rejuvenation. There is much more to do here than to see, with all manner of land and water sports. From **Puerto Vallarta** in the north to **Huatulco** in the south, this coastline is a treasure trove—a golden coast if there ever was one.

A BRIEF HISTORY

Throughout the centuries-old history of Mexico's Pacific Coast, this region has been both a refuge and an important point for conducting trade.

The region's history has some marked differences from the history of Mexico as a country. Although artifacts show that both the Aztec and Olmec pre-Hispanic cultures had a presence in the area, ancient civilizations created no notable settlements here. This fact, coupled with the geography of the region, spared it much of the bloodshed and turmoil of the Spanish conquest. With the imposing Sierra Madre Occidental mountain range running the length of the Pacific coastline, isolating it from the rest of mainland Mexico, the Pacific coast was able to develop at a slower, more tranquil pace.

Most pre-Hispanic tribes that inhabited the coastal areas were peaceful traders and fishermen, and their trading legacy continued well after the conquest of Mexico by Spain. Several of the ports that were important prior to the conquest have—in one way or another—remained on the map as major destinations to this day.

Puerto Vallarta

Puerto Vallarta was launched into the international spotlight when Hollywood director John Huston decided to film the Tennessee Williams' play, *Night of the Iguana*, on nearby **Mismaloya Beach.** Its history, however, runs much deeper than that event. Recent archeological findings show six different cultures lived in the area, with settlements dating back to 300 B.C. The most important was part of the kingdom of Xalisco, centered in the modern state of Nayarit. A marked Aztec influence is also present, probably due to the centuries-long migration of Aztecs from the legendary city of

Movie buffs can visit the ruins of the set built for the 1963 film Night of the Iguana.

Aztlán, on the Pacific coast, to Tenochtitlan, present-day Mexico City. Remains of these cultures can be seen in the **Museo del Río Cuale.**

The first Spaniard to encounter these Nahuatl settlements was Hernán Cortez's nephew, Francisco Cortez de Buenaventura. He arrived at the Jalisco-Nayarit coast in 1524, shortly after the fall of Tenochtitlan. He was met by "…a formidable army of 20,000 warriors, their bows decorated by myriad colored banners…" This impressive assembly earned the fertile Río Ameca Valley (just north of present day Puerto Vallarta) the name Valle de Banderas (Valley of the Banners), and the great bay just in front of the valley became known as Bahía de Banderas.

During colonial days the bay was visited by both Spanish galleons and pirate ships looking for shelter, repairs, or supplies. It was during this time that foreign navigators referred to the bay as Humpback Bay, or Bahía de las Jorobadas, because of the large number of humpback whales that appeared—and still appear—every winter.

In the early 1800s gold and silver were found in the Sierra Madre Mountains, spurring an explosive growth of mining towns, including **Talpa de Allende** and **San Sebastián.** The mines needed salt to process the ore, and an enterprising man named Guadalupe Sánchez found the perfect location for this by the mouth of the Río Cuale. He and his family became the salt suppliers for the Cuale and San Sebastián silver mines. Others arrived to take part in this lucrative trade, and in 1851 the village, called *Puerto Las Peñas,* was established.

The village grew steadily, and by 1895 construction began on the church in the town center, **Iglesia de Nuestra Señora de Guadalupe,** named after the Virgin of Guadalupe, patron saint of the town. Sánchez originally founded the town on December 12th, the anniversary of the Virgin's appearance.

As Las Peñas grew, San Sebastián faded. At its peak in the late 1800s, San Sebastián was one of the most productive mining towns in all Mexico, with a population of over 20,000 (today it has fewer than 2,000 residents). In 1912, governmental functions were moved to Las Peñas, and by 1819, Las Peñas was designated as a municipality, and its name changed to Puerto Vallarta.

Without any highways or an airport to connect it to other major cities, Puerto Vallarta remained in secluded tranquility for almost 50 years—until the 1963 filming of *Night of the Iguana.* The Hollywood production attracted the attention of the international media, who came looking for gossip about the torrid romances of the film's legendary stars. *Night of the Iguana*'s biggest star, however, turned out to be the quaint village of Puerto Vallarta.

The movie's leading man, Richard Burton, and his new love, Elizabeth Taylor, were so charmed by the town that they bought homes there, as did director John Huston. Throngs of tourists followed. Many became residents, building homes of their own on the hillsides overlooking the river and bay, creating what is now known as **Gringo Gulch.** Huston's friend, the Mexican architect Guillermo Wulff built most of these homes, giving Puerto Vallarta its defining style of white facades and red tile roofs.

Puerto Vallarta has continued to grow, and has become an important art center. It attracts an increasing number of visitors to its true Mexican ambiance, coupled with a modern resort environment.

Manzanillo and the Costa Alegre

Since its earliest days, Manzanillo has been considered an important trading port. Legend has it that the ancient residents of the area, the *Colimans,* who traded from this port—then known as *Tzalagua*—had contact with Chinese traders years before the arrival of the Spaniards.

When this rumor reached Cortez, he sent his own men to confirm it. The Spaniards named the place *Manzanillo,* and established it as a shipyard and launching point for expeditions across the Pacific. Its bay offered safe anchorage and a good shipbuilding site. Manzanillo saw considerable growth until the mid-1500s, when, in order to centralize trade, Acapulco was declared the only authorized port in Mexico.

The port of Manzanillo continued to quietly exist until 1889, when a railroad connected it inland. Telephone, electricity, drainage, and potable water services followed. These improvements helped transform Manzanillo into the modern port and manufacturing center it is today.

Manzanillo initially drew the interest of international visitors for its excellent fishing. An important annual fishing tournament prompted the construction of modest hotels and condos. In the 1970s, the development, along with the new airport, of the Club Maeva and Las Hadas resorts, with their striking Moorish design, began to bring in a steady flow of tourists. Then the movie *Ten,* starring Bo Derek and Dudley Moore and filmed in Las Hadas, put Manzanillo squarely in the spotlight.

The beaches and coves along the Costa Alegre, were also popular with pirates and Spanish traders 400 years ago. **Melaque** and **Barra de Navidad** were visited in 1523 by Spanish conquistadors in search of a mythical place believed to have an unlimited quantity of pearls, and to be inhabited only by women. A select number of tourists discovered Melaque and Barra de Navidad in the 1950s, and the towns have grown gracefully since.

Ixtapa–Zihuatanejo: From Pre-Hispanic Resort to Modern Paradise

Zihuatanejo's azure waters caught the attention of tourists long before Mexico became a Spanish colonial empire. Legend has it that the Tarascan emperor Caltzonzin built a royal beach retreat on the popular Zihuatanejo beach of **Las Gatas,** somewhere around A.D. 1400. He turned this already tranquil beach into a virtual wading pool by building a breakwater to keep the waters within it completely calm and crystalline. The mysterious Olmecs, from the Gulf Coast of Mexico, left their unmistakable influence here around 1000 B.C., evidenced by ceramics featuring jaguar-like and Negroid features. Today, some of these may be seen in the **Museo Arqueológico de la Costa Grande** in Zihuatanejo.

In the early 1500s, Aztecs conquered the province of

Revisit colonial Mexico in San Sebastián—once a bustling mining town.

Coyuca, located between present-day Zihuatanejo and the Coyuca lagoon, and established a coastal capital, which they called *Zihuatlan,* "Place of Women," named for the local matriarchal society. Residents today claim that the place was named for the beauty of the women, and means, "place of beautiful women."

Zihuatanejo was claimed for the Spanish crown by Juan Alvarez Chico in 1522. The town and port saw little action during colonial days and it slumbered quietly, hosting a few lost galleons and pirate ships that happened to stop for repairs or supplies. Local lore tells how one such ship, upon returning from its travels to China, lost hundreds of rolls of silk. The name *La Ropa* ("the Clothing") was given to the beach where the silk later washed ashore.

It wasn't until over 400 years later, in the mid-1960s, that this quiet village was awakened with the development of Ixtapa. FONATUR (Mexico's national fund for tourism development) chose this location because of its 7.5 km (5 miles) of pristine beaches, located near a picturesque village. Today Zihuatanejo and Ixtapa meld into a complementary combination that offers the best of both worlds: the quirky character of Zihuatanejo and the deluxe mega-development of Ixtapa.

Acapulco: Colonial Gateway to the Orient and Playground to the Stars

Many regard Acapulco as the original Mexican beach resort with its glimmering beaches and glitzy nightlife. Yet its history extends far beyond its present-day appeal—artifacts found here date back to 2500 B.C. Inhabitants of this zone are known to have traded with several cultures, possibly including the Polynesians. There is clear evidence of trade with the Tarascan, Mixtec, and Zapotec empires that extended to the north and south of Acapulco prior to Mexico's conquest by Spain.

In 1528, the Spanish Crown claimed Acapulco, and established it as the departure point for a trade route to the Orient. A later decree gave Acapulco exclusivity as the only authorized port on the Pacific coast, and for 200 years, it was the unrivaled trading center of Pacific Mexico. The yearly arrival of the *Nao de China*, a galleon that sailed to Manila and back during these years, was the occasion for an annual merchant fair that drew traders from all over the colony.

Before long, pirates heard about the riches brought to Acapulco—the port was visited both by Sir Francis Drake and the British pirate, Thomas Cavendish. Cavendish eventually captured the *Nao* (1587) and got away with 1.2 million in gold. To guard the port from these attacks, the Spaniards built the impressive **Fuerte de San Diego** in 1616. Although an earthquake destroyed it in 1776, the fort was rebuilt in 1783, and today houses a small but interesting museum.

The *Nao* trade route continued until the early 1800s, when José María Morelos y Pavón, a hero of Mexico's War of Independence, took over Acapulco and stopped the trade, sending the town into a century-long respite, a hiatus that ended only when the Mexican government paved the highway between Mexico City and Acapulco. The beautiful beaches of Acapulco Bay immediately lured Mexico City's elite, and the metamorphosis began, from

Now a museum, Fuerte de San Diego once guarded the port from pirate attacks.

Smooth sailing on an ocean of sunlight—another day well spent in Mexico!

slumbering trading port into the "Pearl of the Pacific," as the media came to know it in the 1930s.

The first airplanes from the US began to arrive in the mid-1930s, and with them came a bevy of notorious visitors, from movie stars to presidents, writers to millionaires. Acapulco became the playground for the rich and famous. Glitzy hotels went up in a hurry, supported by new boulevards, power plants, and a superhighway. Acapulco's peak was the 1940s to 1960s. Celebrated images included Frank Sinatra and Ava Gardner sipping margaritas while watching cliff divers at **La Quebrada,** President Eisenhower meeting Mexico's President López Mateos for a summit conference in a new high rise hotel, and Johnny Weissmuller swimming laps in the Flamingos Hotel pool overlooking Acapulco Bay.

Since those glory days Acapulco has aged—maybe not quite as gracefully as its fans would have hoped. However, the "Perla del Pacífico" still attracts scores of vacationers, who are still regaled by old stories about the rich and famous, told by seasoned waiters as they serve pool-side drinks with a weathered but unwavering smile.

Puerto Escondido and Huatulco

Even though Puerto Escondido is the more mature tourist destination of the two, Huatulco has the deepest historical roots. The Aztecs and *Chichimecs* (a Nahuatl-speaking warrior community) knew Huatulco as an important trading port long before the arrival of the Spanish conquistadors.

The name *Huatulco* is of Aztec origin and means "land where a tree is worshipped," reflecting the intriguing legend of the "Santa Cruz de Huatulco" ("Sacred Cross of Huatulco"). When the Spaniards arrived at Huatulco in the late 1530s, the local Indians showed them a massive cross by the edge of the shore that they worshipped. A legend arose that the cross may have been left by an ancient saint—perhaps even the Apostle Thomas—some fifteen centuries earlier. The cross remained during the Spanish conquest and even survived an attempt to destroy it by the pirate Cavendish. In 1612 Bishop Juan de Cervantes took part of the cross to the capital city of Oaxaca and used it as the foundation of a replica, which today stands in the main altar of the cathedral. Another piece was set in silver and sent to the Vatican.

For centuries the bays of Huatulco basked quietly under the sun. Then, in the mid-1970s, FONATUR turned its eyes towards the southern coast of Oaxaca and started a mega-development, scheduled for completion in 2020, on the nine bays of Huatulco.

Puerto Escondido was established in 1928 as a port for shipping coffee. Its importance diminished as coffee shipments began to be transported by truck. In the 1960s tourists discovered the town after it was connected to other coastal towns by Highway 200. With its renowned offshore break, Puerto Escondido became the ultimate destination for backpackers, flower children, surfers looking for the perfect wave, and those attracted by natural beauty and the laid-back pace. True escapists preferred to continue south and visit **Puerto Angel,** a fishing village that was Oaxaca's busiest port for a brief period in the 1870s, before reverting back to its peaceable ways.

Historical Landmarks

2500 B.C. First evidence of trading along the Pacific coast, near Acapulco.

1000–300 B.C. Flourishing of the Olmecs, mysterious mother-culture of pre-Hispanic Mexico.

300 B.C.–A.D. 1600 Important pre-Hispanic settlements in and around Puerto Vallarta and the Valle de Banderas.

1400–1500 Tarascan Indians build and use royal beach resort in Las Gatas, close to present-day Zihuatanejo.

1519–1521 Conquest of Mexico for Spain by Hernán Cortez.

1522 Gonzalo de Sandoval arrives at Manzanillo Bay looking for safe harbor. Juan Alvarez Chico claims coastal lands around Zihuatanejo for Spain.

1524 Francisco Cortez de Buenaventura arrives at the Jalisco-Nayarit coast.

1527 Capitán Alvaro Saavedra sails to China from Zihuatanejo.

1528 Acapulco claimed for the Spanish crown.

1532 Puerto San Agustín, in Huatulco's westernmost bay, established by the Spaniards.

1535 Cortez, in pursuit of a Portuguese fleet, arrives in Manzanillo and christens Bahía de Santiago.

1540 Mexico's first Viceroy, Antonio de Mendoza, disembarks in Barra de Navidad.

1559 King Felipe II of Spain turns Barra de Navidad into royal shipyard.

1561 Acapulco becomes the only port of entry on the Pacific by royal decree.

1565 Father André de Urdaneta finds trading route to China. First *Nao* with goods from the Orient arrives in Acapulco.

1579–1587 The Pacific coast is raided by British pirates.

1616–1783 Acapulco builds the Fort of San Diego.

1801–1821 Pacific trade in Acapulco closed down. Gold and silver found in the Sierra Madre Mountains; mining towns flourish.

1810 The war for independence from Spain begins in central Mexico.

1821 Mexico is declared an independent country.

1851 Guadalpe Sánchez establishes the village of Puerto Las Peñas, today Puerto Vallarta.

1876–1910 Mexico is ruled by Porfirio Díaz, whose elitist government promotes foreign investment, and develops the railroad system.

1910–1917 The Mexican Revolution. Revolutionary leaders ask for new presidential reelections and social reforms. A new constitution is drafted.

1918 Puerto Vallarta is designated a municipality.

1927–1928 New highway brings vacationers to Acapulco from Mexico City. Puerto Escondido is established as a coffee shipping port.

1935–1952 Hollywood turns its attention to Acapulco as preferred vacation spot to the stars. Development of Acapulco by President Miguel Alemán.

1959 US–Mexico summit in Acapulco.

1950–1960 Manzanillo's harbor is modernized and deepened.

1963 Filming of *The Night of The Iguana* draws attention to Puerto Vallarta.

1973–1980 FONATUR invests to develop Ixtapa, located south of Zihuatanejo.

1970–1980 International attention to Manzanillo with the opening of Las Hadas and Maeva and the filming of *Ten*.

1988–2000 FONATUR invests to develop Huatulco and its bays. Development/tourism continues in the area.

WHERE TO GO

PUERTO VALLARTA

Puerto Vallarta's mix of small-town charm and sophisticated services seems to captivate its visitors—it has the highest rate of return visitors of any beach resort in Mexico. It's easy to understand why: The town itself has a picture-postcard appeal —whitewashed houses with red-tile roofs and balconies filled with flowers sit along neat rows of cobblestone streets—and the residents here are renown for their gentle friendliness and understated hospitality. Essentially, Puerto Vallarta is a place where it's easy to feel both relaxed and welcome.

In recent years there has been a significant shift away from the traditional attractions of sunny beaches and generous margaritas to an outstanding array of ecologically sensitive excursions and soft adventures. With the Sierra Madre mountains dominating the eastern horizon, Vallarta sits at the center of 26 miles of beaches that border Banderas Bay, giving it a natural appeal. The varied geography attracts hikers, mountain bikers, sea kayakers, whale-watchers, and divers.

The cultural scene has blossomed as well, with Vallarta— as it is called by the locals—now considered among the country's leading art centers. Especially during the winter months, an almost constant succession of gallery openings and exhibitions attracts creative talent from throughout the Americas. The culinary community has taken numerous awards and accolades back to this seaside town, where more than 250 restaurants offer gourmands their own piece of paradise. Yet what makes this place overwhelmingly attractive is its total lack of pretense and completely comfortable ambiance—it remains down-to-earth, genuinely casual, and simply irresistible.

Though some travelers have expressed concern that Vallarta has grown too much in recent years, the town's geography has imposed clear boundaries, allowing development to gradually expand to the north and south of the central downtown area. Within the town itself, the city government has strict guidelines that ensure the architectural integrity of Vallarta, and in recent years has implemented a successful campaign to maintain the cleanliness of the town.

The expansion in services has been welcome. Along with the exceptional range of dining options and galleries, Vallarta has a bounty of new shops and services, with a sizzling nightlife accented by an excellent live music scene. Taxis are plentiful and inexpensive, as are public buses, making it easy to explore this paradise.

Visitors fall hopelessly in love with Puerto Vallarta's picture-postcard appeal—another blue sky over the marina.

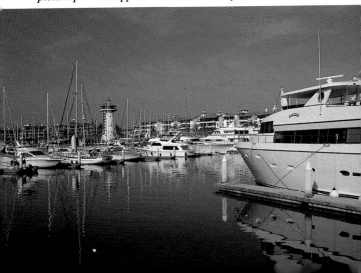

Neighborhoods

Yes, Puerto Vallarta is still small enough to charm. It neatly divides itself into five key areas. Knowing the particulars of each area, helps you select a place to stay that best fits your preferences.

Nuevo Vallarta is found to the north of the Puerto Vallarta international airport, and is actually located in a different state, Nayarit. A planned community, it has evolved into a sister destination of Puerto Vallarta, with ultra-modern hotels, many of them all-inclusive, dominating the wide, beautiful, stretch of beach. This area has a secluded sense of privacy; however, to date, it offers little in the way of dining, shopping, or nightlife outside the hotels. A new festival shopping center, slated to open in the summer of 2000, should increase these options, and transportation into Puerto Vallarta—about 30 minutes by taxi—is readily available. Nuevo Vallarta is also the place to kayak a lagoon or swim with dolphins.

Located just north of downtown, **Marina Vallarta** is the site of modern hotels and wide beaches. It is a resort within a resort, with a championship golf course, ample tennis facilities, and an exclusive marina filled with yachts, sailing vessels, and charter boats. Surrounding the marina are numerous bou-

Stroll along El Centro's malecón, where public sculptures line the walkway.

tiques, restaurants, and travel agencies, plus all types of services to accommodate arriving cruisers. Condominiums, many available for vacation rental, surround the marina as well. This fashionable neighborhood is a favorite with families, and offers the best array of activities and entertainment for the younger traveler—including a water park and mammoth video arcade and entertainment center. Since this development sits on a swampy area that has been filled in, the beaches in Marina Vallarta are less attractive than those in other areas of town, and are occasionally very rocky. The grand hotels make up for this with their dazzling pools, but anyone whose heart is set on true "beach time" should consider another option.

> In Puerto Vallarta, use care in crossing the streets, especially when you see one of the public buses. They seem to regularly race one another, and speed combined with their sheer size results in several fatalities each year.

Vallarta's original hotels were constructed along the stretch of wide, soft sandy strand that extends from the airport into the central downtown area. Along the **Hotel Zone,** there's an ample mix of excellent hotels, and this area is also a great place for recreational watersports and convenient to Vallarta's many treasures. This is also the section of town where the **Terminal Marítima** (Marine Terminal) is located, docking point for cruise ships as well as the numerous excursion boats.

El Centro, the historic downtown area, is known for its traditional white buildings, cobblestone streets, and the **malecón,** the broad seaside walkway bordered by Vallarta's most populated restaurants and bars, and the centerpiece of local life and many visitor photos. Sunday evenings in particular—the traditional evening for a family stroll—are perfect for people watching. All along the malecón, public **sculptures** are dotted, many backed by local legends or lore. The recently installed grouping of sea fantasy sculptures by Mexican master Alejandro Colunga regularly attracts a crowd—sitting on, climbing over, or simply gazing upon these whimsical works of art. This is home for most of the businesses and galleries. Also known as **Viejo Vallarta** it is comprised of the signature cobblestone village extending to the north and south of the Cuale River, and it exemplifies Mexico at its traditional best.

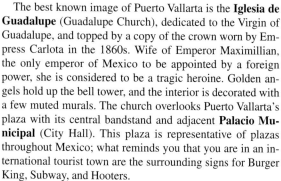

¿Habla inglés?
Do you speak English?

The best known image of Puerto Vallarta is the **Iglesia de Guadalupe** (Guadalupe Church), dedicated to the Virgin of Guadalupe, and topped by a copy of the crown worn by Empress Carlota in the 1860s. Wife of Emperor Maximillian, the only emperor of Mexico to be appointed by a foreign power, she is considered to be a tragic heroine. Golden angels hold up the bell tower, and the interior is decorated with a few muted murals. The church overlooks Puerto Vallarta's plaza with its central bandstand and adjacent **Palacio Municipal** (City Hall). This plaza is representative of plazas throughout Mexico; what reminds you that you are in an international tourist town are the surrounding signs for Burger King, Subway, and Hooters.

Just beyond the plaza is the **Cuale River,** and in its center, a shady retreat—an **island,** found between the two traffic bridges. Birds twitter, men read the papers over a cup of coffee, and a little girl plays with an iguana outside a shop that sells the same reptiles stuffed. At the western end of the island, the small **Museo Río Cuale** features archeological artifacts found in the region. Adjoining the upper bridge, the municipal **mercado** (market) has a range of handicrafts for sale, with traditional foods sold on the second floor.

Overlooking the river, and set back behind the church, is the neighborhood known as **Gringo Gulch,** site of the famed

There is no better way to while away an afternoon than strolling the beach with a cool breeze and rhythmic tide.

Burton-Taylor homes. A pink-hued replica of the Bridge of Sighs connects these two villas. Depending on the prevalent mood of the caretaker, you may be able to view the interior—eerily preserved in a museum-type manner—by forking over US$5.

South of El Centro, yet still considered to be a part of Viejo Vallarta, is the area alternately known as "**Los Muertos**" and "**Zona Romántica.**" The neighborhood is named for the main beach in town, Los Muertos (the Dead)—however, the city fathers prefer a kinder, gentler nomenclature, and have unsuccessfully tried to rename it "Zona Romántica," and the beach, "Playa del Sol" (just so you'll know when you see the many street signs). From family-run beachfront hotels to eclectic inns poised on the surrounding hills, here is where you feel the essence of Vallarta's charms—the area preferred by independent travelers and repeat visitors. New sidewalk cafés, book-

A tribute to the Virgin of Guadalupe on the beach— a symbol of Mexico's faith.

stores, and martini bars have popped up along the main road, Olas Altas, giving it a decidedly bohemian, funky feel. This part of town also is home to "Restaurant Row" (along Basilio Badillo) and Rockin' Row (Ignacio L. Vallarta, just beyond the southbound bridge). This perpendicular meeting of streets contains something for every taste and budget, in both dining and nightlife.

Immediately south of Viejo Vallarta is the fashionable residential neighborhood of **Conchas Chinas,** with numerous villas for rent, and a few hotels set into the cliffside. Extending from Conchas Chinas along the **South Shore,** the landscape changes to dramatic mountains that tumble toward the sea. Tucked into the private coves of this coast, you'll find a collection of full-service hotels made to order for honeymoons and romantic escapes. At the end of this stretch of shore, you'll come to **Mismaloya Bay,** where you can still climb up the ridge to the ruins of the set built for the *Night of the Iguana.*

DAY TRIPS FROM PUERTO VALLARTA

☛ Yelapa and the Southern Beaches

A boat ride away from Vallarta, **Yelapa** offers a Robinson Crusoe–style getaway for day trips or overnight stays. No

30

electricity and no roads keep it a secluded, funky beach community, populated in part by ex-pats and artists. The other south shore beaches are **Las Animas** and **Quimixto,** appropriate for day trips only. These two offer palapa beach dining, and as tropical a setting as you can dream up. Las

Mexico's "Guadalupe"

Though Mexicans traditionally disagree when it comes to politics or economics, there is a saying that "Todos los Mexicanos somos Guadalupanos" ("All Mexicans believe in the Virgin of Guadalupe"). The Virgin of Guadalupe is both the patron saint of Mexico, and of Puerto Vallarta. Each year, the anniversary of her miraculous appearance to the peasant Juan Diego is celebrated on December 12. What makes this Virgin so meaningful in the Mexican culture is her dark skin—which helped the Catholic church enormously in converting the indigenous inhabitants of Mexico. Her first appearance was at the site of the former Aztec temple to the mother of the gods, further adding a unifying connection between the two spiritual worlds.

One of the most colorful of the *Festival Guadalupano* celebrations takes place in Puerto Vallarta. From December 1st through 12th, the whole town participates; and local businesses, neighborhoods, and civic groups organize processions to the **Iglesia de Nuestra Señora de Guadalupe**, where an exact replica of the miraculous image is venerated, to pay homage. These processions are complete with Aztec dancers, strolling mariachis, floats, and fireworks. The most impressive *peregrinaciones* are held on the 12th, the Día de la Virgen, with the processions of charros and mariachis, with everyone—even the youngest toddlers—dressed in their best garb. Another moving ritual is the solemn, silent procession of "Los Favorecidos"—all those who have received blessings or for whom the Virgin has worked miracles.

31

Animas has the better beach for swimming and sunning, but Quimixto has a beautiful waterfall that you can reach by walking about 30 minutes inland along a well-marked trail. The coves surrounding Quimixto are also noted by divers and snorkelers for their excellent underwater vistas. These three beaches may all be reached by excursion boat, or for longer, less structured stays, take the water taxi from either the Rosita (malecón) , or Los Muertos pier.

Northern Beaches and Towns

Further north beyond Nuevo Vallarta are a succession of small towns and relatively undeveloped beaches, in easy reach by car. Just a few kilometers to the east, traditional Mexican farming life goes its unhurried way up steep mountain roads where views can be superb and well worth the extra drive. The simple and the sensational seem to coexist so easily here.

Bucerías is a breezy beach community known for its fresh oysters and the palapa restaurants on its wide, white-sand

Paradise found—The toughest part of visiting Puerto Vallarta and Acapulco is leaving…

beach. Independent small hotels and rental homes provide overnight accommodations.

At the very northern top of Banderas Bay, where the bay, the Pacific Ocean, and Sea of Cortez meet, lies **Punta Mita.** Long known as a place of high spiritual energy, this is now the home of a new Four Seasons Resort and Jack Nicklaus golf course, with more high-end development planned. **Sayulita** and **San Francisco** are two intriguing towns located north of Banderas Bay, on the Pacific Ocean. These two beach towns offer quiet, rustic alternatives to Puerto Vallarta. Both offer limited, mostly casual beach dining, and are popular with surfers and backpackers.

Mountain Villages

Throughout the 17th century, the picturesque mountain village of **San Sebastián** was one of the most populated towns in Mexico, renown for its mining activity. Now, it resembles a quiet ghost town, locked in time. Limited overnight accommodations are available. Notable is the Hacienda Jalisco, the old center of mining activity, and now an inn run by ex-pat Bud Acord. He has welcomed John Huston, Richard Burton, and Elizabeth Taylor among his guests.

Another mountain town located in the high Sierra, east of Puerto Vallarta is **Talpa.** Accessible by a short flight or a long and winding mountain road, this traditional town is known as the home of the Virgin of Talpa, one of Mexico's most noted religious icons, and a popular pilgrimage destination.

COSTA ALEGRE AND MANZANILLO

Costa Alegre

The coastal area between Puerto Vallarta and Manzanillo, with its hundreds of coves and pristine beaches backed by mountainous jungle terrain, is commonly known as **Costa Alegre**, or **Costa Careyes**. This area has become a haven for

Abierto **Open**
Cerrado **Closed**

both discriminating travelers looking for super-exclusive resorts and budget-conscious tourists seeking secluded beaches off the beaten path. A collection of upscale and unusual resorts, plus two stellar oceanside golf courses are bringing attention to this exquisite section of coast.

A large, all-inclusive hotel and an adjacent holistic resort have most of lovely **Tenacatita Bay** to themselves. There are campsites on beaches fringed with cocoa palms down side roads all along the coast. The road rises and falls, twists and turns as it crosses ridge after jungle ridge, sloping steeply westward like the backs of great green animals leaning down to drink from the sea.

Barra de Navidad, and **San Patricio–Melaque** are located at opposite ends of a 5-km (3-mile) beach backed by a lagoon. Both little towns have a languid atmosphere and have remained small enough to enable you to really know the place within the first few hours after arrival, yet also offer a pleasant selection of accommodations at very reasonable prices. Barra de Navidad exudes a funky charm, and is as casual and rustic a Mexican seaside town as you're likely to find. Unpaved streets and palapa-topped seafood shacks offer an intriguing contrast to the large and luxurious Grand Bay Hotel and golf course, just a 50-cent panga ride away on Isla Navidad. The combination of an idyllic resort and spicy local color is beguiling.

Manzanillo

Manzanillo is a dichotomous place—it is both Mexico's busiest commercial seaport and a tranquil, traditional town of simple seafood restaurants, shell shops, and a few salsa clubs.

For years, Manzanillo has been known for its wide, curving beaches, legendary sport-fishing, and a highly praised diversity of dive sites. Now however, between its own golf links and those located up the northern coast, it is rivaling Los Cabos as the emerging golf capital of Mexico.

Manzanillo has an enticingly tropical geography, comprised of vast groves of tall palms, abundant mango trees, and successive coves graced with smooth sand beaches. To the north, mountains blanketed with palms rise alongside the shoreline.

With rustic local charm and an idyllic ocean resort, Barra de Navidad is sure to please.

And over it all lies the veneer of perfect weather—balmy temperatures and year-round sea breezes. Even the approach by plane into Manzanillo showcases the promise of a perfect vacation—you fly in over the beach and golf course.

A visit to the town itself is as mandatory as a stroll in the **plaza**—a ritual here for the locals. Around sunset, they gather and gossip on park benches, while hundreds of birds congregate on the surrounding telephone wires, cooing and calling out until, eventually, handfuls of rice, sold by the plastic baggie-full around the plaza's perimeter, are tossed out to them. Children chase after the birds, stopping just short of the splashing fountains, their laughter competing with the chimes of the church bells. In the background, multicolor houses in many hues cascade down the surrounding hillsides, and a game of pickup basketball is played on the public court that fronts the harbor. Located almost behind the city, stretching south along the coast for miles, is the **Laguna de Cuyutlán,** a stellar birdwatching site.

As you depart the downtown area, you pass by the **Museo Universitario de Arqueología de Manzanillo** (University Museum of Archeology in Manzanillo)—easily the region's most impressive collection of regional historical artifacts—and the large commercial wharves before reaching the turnoff to **Las Brisas.** This long stretch of golden sand beach on a peninsula separates Manzanillo bay from the **San Pedrito lagoon,** another birdwatching haven. Las Brisas Peninsula is where several older, budget hotels are located, along with a handful of recommendable restaurants. In general, this section of Manzanillo is quite run-down, having never recovered from damage caused by a 1995 earthquake.

About seven miles west of downtown, lies the **Península de Santiago,** Manzanillo's best known landmark. For many travelers, this town is synonymous with the famed all-white world of **Las Hadas** ("the Fairies") and its adjoining golf course. Set on a southern promontory of Santiago Peninsula, Las Hadas gazes across Manzanillo Bay

Manzanillo boasts one of the region's finest collections of historical artifacts.

to the town, but is a world apart in character. Its Moorish architecture, which looks something like a setting for Arabian Nights, became renown as the place where Bo Derek showed her appreciation for Ravel's bolero in the movie *Ten*. Las Hadas was built in the 1970s by the Bolivian tin multimillionaire Antinor Patiño as a private, super-exclusive resort

> In Mexico fair-haired people are referred to as güero or güera, so if you are blonde and female you will hear lots of "güera, güerita" as you walk by. Understand it's intended as a compliment—though at times it may sound like a sleazy catcall.

and a respite from Acapulco's excessive glitz. Its presence spawned construction up and down the adjoining beaches, making Santiago Peninsula the most desirable address in town, especially for visitors to Manzanillo.

At one time, the **La Mantarraya golf course** on the Santiago Peninsula was considered among the top 100 courses in the world, but it's been upshot by newer entries. Local legend has it that when the course was under construction, pre-Hispanic ceramic figurines, idols, and beads were dug up at the spot where the 14th hole now lies; it is believed to have been an important ancient burial site. The nearby **El Tesoro** (the Treasure) beach is also the subject of local lore—many believe this beach still may hold buried treasure from Spanish galleons, whose crews used the harbor during the 16th century.

On the other side of Santiago lies a succession of locally popular beaches, including the long stretch known as **Playa Olas Altas,** named after the high waves that regularly break here. Just beyond is **Playa Miramar,** prized by bodysurfers and boogie borders for its challenging waves. The adjacent beachfront has a collection of colorful beach restaurants for enjoying a casual day at the beach.

IXTAPA/ZIHUATANEJO

These neighboring towns, when combined, provide the quintessential Mexican beach experience. **Ixtapa** is a planned resort with modern hotels and slick shopping, while **Zihuatanejo**—referred to by locals as *Zihua* (pronounced *see-wah*)—is the original rustic beach town.

Zihuatanejo

Zihuatanejo became popular among beachcombers from abroad because it had what they wanted: a sparkling bay divided into intimate stretches of sand by outcroppings of rock and wooded knolls, plus simple pleasures that included swimming, sunning, and the freshest of fruit and seafood. Cheap beer and rum were an added bonus.

During the 1960s Zihuatanejo's charm attracted numerous European visitors who have become regulars of this no-longer-rustic beach resort. A number have been so taken by its balmy beauty that they decided to make Zihua their permanent home, giving it a continental air.

The town embraces the beautiful Bay of Zihuatanejo with the downtown area to the north, and the beautiful long beach of **Playa Larga** to the east. The heart of Zihuatanejo is the waterfront boardwalk, **Paseo del Pescador,** also referred to as the malecón. Unlike most Mexican towns, Zihuatanejo doesn't have a main square or Plaza de Armas. Instead, the centerpiece of the downtown promenade is **La Cancha,** a basketball court, that serves as the gathering place for bands that play on Sunday evenings, and vendors who offer tamales and elotes (corn) for sale, along with sweet homemade popsicles flavored with chocolate, cinnamon, or vanilla.

La Cancha fronts the **Playa Municipal,** where local fishermen pull their small boats onto the sand, making it an excellent place to people-watch and take in the daily village life. Many of downtown Zihuatanejo's store-lined streets are designated as *zona peatonal* (pedestrian zone), making it especially welcoming to those who prefer to explore on foot.

Zihuatanejo also has one of the better archeological museums on the Pacific coast. The **Museo Arqueológico de la Costa Grande,** located near the eastern end of Paseo del Pescador, traces the history of this area from pre-Hispanic times, when the place was known as *Zihuatlán*, through the colonial era.

Playa Las Gatas guarantees hours of under-the-sun fun for the whole family

Most of the exhibits show that the area was an important trading zone for centuries, with items from far-off cultures such as the Teotihuacan and Toltec.

Past the municipal beach lies **Playa La Madera,** once a loading point for lumber—hence the name, which means "wood beach." It has fine grayish-white sand, and the swells that enter it break suddenly into small waves that roll gently and then recede, with little undertow. This beach's calm waters are ideal for children and easy swimming. A few beachside restaurants offer drinks and snacks, and the ever-present beach vendors offer their wares to the sunning tourists.

Playa La Ropa is Zihuatanejo's most popular beach, a long crescent of golden sand that stretches south past La Madera beach and receives the gentle breezes that blow in from the bay. The beach was named for the yards of colorful cloth that washed ashore centuries ago, following a trading galleon's wreck. The waves are generally too gentle and quick-breaking for surfing, but you will find jet-skis, catamarans, and wind-surf boards for rent here. Several beachfront restaurants offer

Days of the Dead

A celebration that is particularly interesting in Mexico is the *Día de los Santos Inocentes* and *Día de Muertos* . Only in Mexico will you find a full two days of celebrations focusing completely on the mysticism of death. This part of Mexican culture reflects the prevailing attitude regarding things you can't avoid—if you can't help the situation, you might as well make a party of it. The way Mexicans see it, death is more than an unavoidable event, it is a mystical occurrence, and a passage to a better place where the deceased continue to keep a watchful eye over the loved ones they've left behind. November 1st honors children who have died. On the eve of November 2nd, departed souls get a chance to come back and join their loved ones. While the most elaborate celebrations are held in the smaller towns of Mexico, such as Talpa, and San Sebastián and the coastal village of Melaque, you will find *altares*, altars put up at the gravesides to welcome the souls of the dead, throughout Pacific Mexico. These altars hold the favorite foods and drinks of the deceased, plus photos and flowers, usually marigolds. Each year, Puerto Vallarta's City Hall hosts an altar-decorating competition and exhibition. All-night vigils are held, at home or in the cemetery, and traditional foods are prepared, including *pan de muerto*, a sweet bread decorated with bone-shaped pieces of bread, candy, and chocolate skulls. In the coastal regions this is more of a private, family celebration than it is in the interior towns of Mexico.

food and drinks. Alongside this beach you will find lovely, and rather exclusive, hotels and B&Bs.

Playa Las Gatas, once a walled pre-Hispanic wading pool, earned its name from the whiskered nurse sharks that used to frequent the surrounding wall. Today Las Gatas is the most pleasant beach for swimming and children's activities. The coral beach has exceptionally clear waters, with little or no surf,

> *Buenas tardes.*
> **Good afternoon/evening.**

and practically no undertow. Located across the bay from Playa La Ropa, it is easily reached by a short ride aboard small, shaded boats that run from the **Muelle** (the town pier) every 10-minutes. Open air restaurants, some fancier than others, offer local delicacies, including extraordinarily fresh pink-tongued clams. Las Gatas is a departing point for dive trips to some excellent sites.

Although Zihuatanejo has grown more sophisticated, with trendy boutiques and candle-lit restaurants that overlook the bay, those looking for a more developed tourist resort should take advantage of the luxury accommodations of Ixtapa. A new highway, finished in 1999, connects the 6km (4 miles) between Zihua and Ixtapa.

Ixtapa

In a pristine setting of great natural beauty, this pre-planned FONATUR development rose to glory in the late 1960s. Ixtapa has become known for its manicured luxury along its long stretch of beach. It also offers challenging golf, tennis, windsurfing, and all the amenities of a top resort, without the traffic and hustle of a place the size of Acapulco. Its hotels are ultramodern, yet were designed to fit harmoniously into the tropical environment. Minibuses shuttle back and forth between the two towns, or you can rent a moped for more independence.

The inland side of Ixtapa is marked by the 18-hole **Club de Golf Ixtapa.** Nearly everything in Ixtapa lies along the main boulevard, **Paseo Ixtapa,** which runs parallel to the hotel-lined main beach, **Playa Palmar.** This beach offers 4¹/₂ km (3 miles) of beautiful white sand and deep azure waters. Even though the beach faces the open sea, there are several spots where offshore rocks and islands quiet the surf and make the waters suitable for swimming. The undertow here, however, is usually quite strong, and extreme caution should be taken. For a stunning view of this beach, ride the cable car to El Faro restaurant, located on the southern end of the beach, upstairs from the Pacifica Hotel. At the far end of Paseo Ixtapa lies **Marina Ixtapa,** with fine restaurants, private yacht slips, and the **Marina Ixtapa Golf Course.**

Ixtapa also has its share of trendy shops and boutiques, plus lively nightlife, and refined dining. A bicycle track begins at the marina, continues around the golf course, and heads on towards the northern beach of **Playa Linda.**

The first beach in Ixtapa, coming from Zihua is **Playa**

Hermosa, which can only be accessed through the Westin Hotel. This small beach is dramatically framed by rock formations. The surf varies seasonally from minimal to quite rough, and has become somewhat of a private beach for Westin's guests.

Playa Linda is located 12km (8 miles) north of Ixtapa. This is a long beach with

Set sails for Isla Ixtapa— an island paradise you won't soon forget…

golden sands that seem to stretch endlessly to the north. It is the primary out-of-town beach, with water sports equipment rentals, fishing charters, and horseback riding. The ferry to **Isla Ixtapa** leaves from the jetty located on the southern end of Playa Linda.

Isla Ixtapa is among the area's most memorable sites, and is easily reached by boat. The island's

> At the beach, ask for a *michelada* instead of a cold beer. This drink consists of cold beer served over ice with lime juice and salt—a good way to lower the your alcohol intake. The ice waters down the beer and the salt helps keep you from dehydrating.

small beaches have managed to maintain their natural beauty, despite the throngs of visitors that land daily. Palapa proprietors do a great job of keeping all trash off the island. It is a perfect place to spend the day enjoying the beach, swimming, snorkeling, and eating fresh fish and seafood at any one of a dozen or so palapa restaurants. Hundreds of colored fish dart among the rocks just offshore. Boats ride back to the mainland every few minutes, with the last boat leaving around 5pm (always double-check the departure time of the last boat).

DAY TRIPS FROM ZIHUATANEJO AND IXTAPA

Another excellent spot to spend a day away from the more crowded beaches of Ixtapa and Zihuatanejo is **Playa Larga.** A beautiful, uncrowded beach that stretches for miles, Playa Larga is located south of the bay, between Zihuatanejo and the airport. The surf here is usually quite rough and with a strong undertow, so it is not recommended for swimming. However, the many small restaurants that border it make up for this shortfall by offering wading pools that are refilled daily, along with hammocks for lazing under the palapa shades, and fresh fish and seafood accompanied by ice-cold beer. There is also the occasional musical rendering by a wandering beach troubadour.

A countryside visit to **Barra de Potosí,** located 21 km (14 miles) south of Zihuatanejo offers a chance to see a small fishing village, coconut and mango plantations, and a lagoon known for the numerous tropical birds that inhabit it.

Further south along the coast is the small town of **Petatlán** and the **Laguna de San Valentín,** which can also be visited as a day trip from Zihua. Highlights of this trip may include a visit to the small town's museum, the local market where bartering is still practiced, the town's church dating back to the 17th century, and a chance to have lunch on a small island in the lagoon, amid hundreds of tropical birds.

Troncones is a tiny fishing village located 30 km (20 miles) northwest of Ixtapa, where visitors can absolutely escape from it all. There is little more to do here beyond strolling along the beach, swimming, and savoring the fresh local seafood. This place offers several options for overnight stays from an exclusive B&B to RV facilities, as well as camping on the beach. No public buses serve this town, so you'll have to hire a taxi to take you there, and arrange for the same taxi to pick you up when you are ready to return.

ACAPULCO

If beach resorts are made for relaxing, then Acapulco is the exception that proves the rule. Here, the energy is turned up more than a few notches, and, if you do enjoy languid days in the sun, likely it's only to rest up for playful nights at decadent discos or other nocturnal alternatives.

Though Acapulco is, admittedly, past its prime, there are still plenty of reasons to visit and numerous ways to enjoy the famously sunny days there. Acapulco remains Mexico's most traditional resort for those looking for a beach, yet also want to feel as if they've been to Mexico. Where other resorts in Mexico have been accused of being homogenized to meet the

The idyllic sprawl of Acapulco from the bay—a city where daytime is well spent preparing for an evening of adventure.

tastes of North American travelers, Acapulco remains true to her essence, from the cacophony of families filling colorful, public sands, to the classically late nights in glitzy clubs.

And Acapulco has one thing that no other place has—the absolutely stunning view of Acapulco Bay, which, day or night, is an image as memorable as any you'll come across in your travels.

Acapulco is more of a city than other Pacific coastal destinations, with high-rise hotels lined up like dominoes around the edge of the bay. It offers more options for dining, shopping, and other activities than anywhere else along Mexico's western shoreline; many are geared for families.

The one cautionary note concerns the reputed lack of cleanliness in Acapulco, especially in the waters of Acapulco Bay. Great strides have been made in cleaning up the pollution that was widely reported in the 1970s and 1980s. However, the water remains less pristine than in resorts to the north and south, and most visitors—wisely—prefer to swim in hotel pools. A public works program put in place in the 1990s, ACA-Limpia, has also made progress in cleaning up the beaches and other public areas, including the heavily-trafficked Costera. More than 20 powerboat sweepers are dispatched each day to skim any floating debris from the water's surface. More important, needed improvements in infrastructure—estimated at over a billion dollars—are nearing completion, which should also improve the cleanliness of the city and bay.

As it fell out of favor as an international darling, its prices adjusted out of necessity. Now, some exceptional values in hotels and dining can be found, and today Acapulco is considered a value-packed destination, attracting more Mexican national than foreign tourism.

Other new initiatives are also gaining momentum, including new eco-tourism oriented excursions, and a revival of Acapulco's historic center, in a similar fashion to Miami's South Beach district.

Through all the changes that Acapulco has experienced over the years, this sultry diva of a destination continues to seduce visitors, and tempt them into "just one more dance before calling it a night…"

Neighborhoods

Although it stretches for almost 25 km (15.5 miles) around the bay, Acapulco can roughly be divided into three main areas. The historic downtown is located on the northwestern edge of the bay while the Costera, home of the high-rise lineup of hotels and a wide stretch of golden beach, lies in the center. Las Brisas and Acapulco Diamante areas—handily the most exclusive addresses in Acapulco—are found south of Acapulco Bay.

Historic Centro

Also known as **Acapulco Viejo** (Old Acapulco), this intriguing area is the part of Acapulco that originally attracted the glamorous jet-setters of days past, and which, today, is experiencing something of a renaissance. For years, travelers to Acapulco have dismissed this section of town, which includes the Península de las Playas and extends east to Papagayo Park, not knowing what they're missing. Currently, it is where Acapulco's most value-priced hotels are found, along with budget dining choices and the typical businesses and services of any sizable city.

Older buildings here were constructed in various architectural styles, including some classic deco structures, and numerous faux-forties buildings. One of the hidden treasures of this part of town is the **home of Dolores Olmedo,** decorated on the exterior with a colorful tile, stone, and shell mosaic by Mexico's master muralist, **Diego Rivera.** Rivera, who lived here during the two years preceding his death, created the mural in 1956, taking 18 months to complete it. The home remains a private residence and not a museum; however there are additional murals by Rivera inside.

The centerpiece of downtown is its **zócalo** (central plaza), heavily laden with shade trees and bordered by Acapulco's principal church,

The vivid Nuestra Señora de la Soledad stands watch over the downtown zócalo.

Next stop, Caleta Beach — perhaps the most popular beach in Acapulco.

Nuestra Señora de la Soledad, as well as numerous, inexpensive cafés and restaurants. This church is one of the more notable structures in Acapulco The blue onion-like domes are more Russian Orthodox than Roman Catholic in style—in fact, the structure was originally built as a movie set. Every Sunday evening, local bands serenade the plaza's numerous visitors. Across from the plaza is the beach, **Playa Manzanillo,** where sport-fishing charters, as well as pleasure and excursion boats depart.

One of Acapulco's historic landmarks is the **Fuerte de San Diego,** originally built in 1616 to protect against pirate attacks, and later renovated following extensive earthquake damage in 1776. Acapulco's most notable museum, **Museo Histórico de Acapulco,** is now located in this structure, chronicling Acapulco's exotic history as a trading port. The fort is located up a hill and to the right of the zocalo, just off the Costera.

Also near the zócalo are the most authentic shopping experiences—the **Mercado de Artesanías** (Crafts Market) and the **Mercado Municipal,** which sells fresh and prepared food.

Just up the hill behind the zócalo, about ten minutes walking time, is **La Quebrada,** home of the famed cliff-divers. Although the midday and sunset shows are impressive, the most popular exhibitions take place after dark, when the cliff divers plunge from this 130-foot cliff while holding flaming torches. Just around the bend from La Quebrada is **Playa La Angosta,** a sheltered and often deserted cove.

However, **Caleta** and **Caletilla,** coves located south of the zócolo on the Peninsula de las Playas, are the most popular public beaches in Acapulco. They are colorful sites, with palapa-topped beach restaurants, bright-hued passenger boats, water sports–equipment rental stands, and fishermen selling their fresh catch to beachgoers. These side-by-side beaches are separated by a narrow, rocky peninsular, which is the site of the **Mágico Mundo Marino** water park and aquarium.

Roqueta Island sits half a mile across a channel from Caleta and Caletilla beaches, and is the destination for the numerous glass-bottom boats that cruise over a sunken statue of the Virgin of Guadalupe, before circling around this outcropping of rocks. Roqueta is in the process of gaining national status as a protected nature reserve, but today, is only the site of a rather small, dismal zoo with claims that it is the world's only zoo on an island—however, it's not worth disembarking to visit.

Traveling east from the zócalo and Playa Manzanillo are **Playa Los Hornos** and **Playa Hornitos.** Both of these tradi-

At night when you are strolling or dining, you'll be approached by children who want to sell a rose to the "nice couple" or "*la señorita.*" A sharp vendor will hand you the rose and then demand anywhere between 10 and 20 pesos. If you don't feel like buying the rose don't take it—once it's in your hands it's too late. These children are generally "managed" by adults known as *Marías,* and the money mostly goes to the "manager." If you truly feel sorry for the children, bring them toys or clothes on your next trip—buying their flowers just assures their place on the street.

Coyuca Lagoon, a freshwater lagoon popular with waterskiers, is also rich in bird life.

tional beaches offer wide stretches of sand and numerous palapa restaurants where you can pass the day, while enjoying fresh seafood and cold tropical drinks. Hornitos forms the edge of the 52-acre **Papagayo Park,** considered to be the eastern boundary that separates Acapulco Viejo from the newer Hotel Zone.

Located about seven miles north of town, accessible by public bus or taxi, is the northern beach area, **Pie de la Cuesta,** with its scenic sandbar and numerous seaside restaurants. The adjacent **Coyuca Lagon** was the shooting location for *Rambo II,* filmed in 1985, one of more than 250 movies that have been shot in Acapulco. Even more significant, this tropical estuary is rich with bird life, and has become the focus of current eco-tourism efforts. Bordered by palm trees, the bay at the mouth of this freshwater lagoon is a popular site for water skiing. Boat rides through several canals can stop at Isla de los Pajaros for lunch. Mudbaths and spectacular sunset viewing are additional attractions, and palapa restaurants are available where you can dine. Be aware that the water is very rough, and swimming is not recommended in the open sea.

La Costera Hotel Zone

This popular, lively Hotel Zone borders **Condesa** and **Paraiso** beaches on one side, and the broad main avenue, Costera Miguel Alemán, on the other. It is also known as the Zona Dorado, or Golden Acapulco. This 8 km (5 mile) length of boulevard hugs the edge of the bay, and is lined with towering hotels, shops, restaurants, strip malls, movie theatres, and a string of open-air beach bars. In the evenings, *calendrias*—balloon-draped horse carriages—line up to take passengers for rides.

Among the principal attractions of this area are the 9-hole public Club de Golf Acapulco, the **Acapulco International Center** (considered the grandest convention center in Mexico), and the **Centro Internacional de Convivencia Infantil (CICI)** children's activity park (see page 89).

At the eastern edge of the Zona Dorado is **Playa Icacos,** and the Mexican naval base, **La Base.** Just before reaching La Base, on the beach side of the Costera, is the **Casa de la Cultura,** a small cultural complex with rotating art exhibits and an archeological museum.

Las Brisas and Acapulco Diamante

With its hillsides of cascading villas and luxury homes, this is the most exclusive section of Acapulco. The best selection of gourmet restaurants and the famed cliffside discos, with spectacular views of the twinkling lights of the bay and city, are here.

Las Brisas is more or less defined by the hotel of the same name, with its more than 250 individual guest pools and the pink-and-white theme that extends to the hotel's private fleet of rental jeeps.

Driving further south along the Costera—whose name changes to **Carretera Escénica** (Scenic Highway)—you'll reach the posh residential area of Acapulco Diamante, and the public beach, Playa Marqués. This beach is located in **Puerto Marqués,** a smaller "bay within a bay," and has a clean swimming beach and a row of rustic palapa-topped beach restaurants. The calm waters make it ideal for water skiing and other water sports.

> It is common to see people cross themselves as they walk or ride in front of a church. This is done as a sign of respect, and confirms the deeply ingrained Catholic background of Mexican culture.

Just past here is Puente Diamante, the Acapulco Princess Golf Club, and a row of luxury hotels that fronts the open Pacific Ocean. The airport lies further south along the Carretera.

A DAY TRIP TO TAXCO

Admittedly, Acapulco is not a city brimming over with culture, but located just a few short hours away is one of Mexico's classical colonial treasures, the town of **Taxco.** It's an easy day trip from Acapulco to this famed silver-mining town, and worthwhile for anyone interested in experiencing more of this country's historical past.

The village of Taxco sits atop a hill among the tumbling hillsides of the Sierra Madre Mountains, which were once rich with silver. Though the mines have mostly been tapped out, Taxco's reputation as the Silver City of Mexico remains, due to the skilled workmanship and artistry of local silversmiths in creating silver jewelry and other artifacts.

Atop the rolling hills of the Sierra Madre Mountains stands Taxco, one of Mexico's classic colonial treasures.

The town itself—declared a national monument in 1928—is one of the most picturesque in the country, with narrow, winding cobblestone streets that pass white stucco buildings topped with red-tile roofs, and adorned with flowers tumbling from window boxes. At 5,000 feet elevation, Taxco offers a succession of picturesque views, each seemingly more enchanting than the last.

Among the numerous silversmith shops here, you'll find several landmarks. Most notable is the **Church of San Sebastián and Santa Prisca,** located on **Plaza Borda.** This elaborate church was built by silver magnate Joseph Borda as a show of his appreciation to the town and to the Almighty for the wealth he accumulated here. Additional attractions are the **Museo de Taxco Guillermo Spratling,** featuring a collection of pre-Columbian artifacts, the **Silver Museum,** and the **Casa Humboldt,** which details the past of this historic town.

Taxco is located 275 km (165 miles) north of Acapulco, and can be reached in about three hours by car, traveling the toll road (about US$20). Guided tours traveling by bus are also available through most Acapulco travel agencies or hotel hospitality desks.

PUERTO ESCONDIDO

This coastal town is the ideal place for travelers who are looking for a more laid-back beach village ambiance rather than a "made-for-tourism" resort. It's the best of its kind in Pacific Mexico, with a good selection of independently owned hotels and restaurants, plus a rousing nightlife, and lots of truly adventurous eco-tours.

For years, Puerto Escondido—called simply "Puerto" by the locals—has been known as a surfers' haven, due to the awesome break at **Playa Zicatela,** known as "The Mexican Pipeline." The site of annual international surf competitions during fall swells, it continues to draw those in search of the perfect wave as well as scores of travelers content to gaze at the ocean, soak up the sun,

Time for your midday siesta? Kickback and enjoy the beachside shade.

Highlights Along the Pacific Coast

Acapulco's Discos. The essence of what Acapulco is all about. No visit is complete without a night spent dancing at the light flashing, music blaring, mingling haven discos.

Banderas Bay. Whether it's a cruise to the Marietas Islands, or a sunset sail along Puerto Vallarta's shoreline, the beauty of the bay is best seen from the water.

Fuerte de San Diego. The oldest building in Acapulco, this fort was built in the 17th century to protect against pirate attacks, and today houses a museum of regional history.

Huatulco's bays. A cruise is the absolute best way to see Huatulco's nine beautiful bays.

La Quebrada. a sight not to be missed is Acapulco's famed cliff divers, who plunge 130 feet from a narrow gorge into the ocean every day.

The malecón. Puerto Vallarta's seaside boardwalk has a notable permanent display of sculptures by recognized artists, including Alejandro Colunga and Ramiz Barquet.

Museo Arqueológico de la Costa Grande. an outstanding museum in Zihuatanejo that retraces the history of the area between Zihuatanejo and Acapulco.

Nuestra Señora de Guadalupe Church. Puerto Vallarta's most notable landmark, with its unique crown, held up by angels.

Nuestra Señora de la Soledad. Acapulco's principal church, with its unusual architecture and blue onion-like domes, dominates the shady plaza bordered by cafes and newstands.

Playa Zicatela. In Puerto Escondido, the best waves on the Mexican Pacific coast.

San Sebastián. This mountain village, once Mexico's most important mining center, seems locked in the past—it's a trip back in time.

Sunset sail in Acapulco Bay. The view from the bay lit up at night is absolutely stunning, and an image as memorable as any you'll come across in your travels.

Taxco. With its landmark Iglesia de Santa Prisca, and numerous silversmiths, is an outstanding example of colonial Mexico.

Its back to the beach just after sunset for an evening cocktail and a glimpse of moonlight dancing on the surf.

and chat about the experience over a cold beer or iced *latte*. Puerto Escondido is currently popular with younger, predominately European travelers, and, simply stated , offers the best overall value in a Mexican beach vacation today.

It's easy to get around the central beach and town areas by walking, though bicycle rentals are also a practical option. At the center of town is a curving stretch of beach, **Playa Principal,** where colorful *panga* boats line up offering fishing trips or tours to secluded beaches. The main street that runs parallel to this beach is known as the *Adoquín*, named for the hexagon-shaped interlocking bricks used in its paving. During the morning, traffic is allowed for making deliveries, but after 2pm, it's pedestrians only.

Hotels, shops, restaurants, bars, and travel agencies are all conveniently located here.

Playa Marinero extends from the central beach to the rocky outcropping, **Rocas del Morro,** that marks the beginning of Zicatela and its impressive waves. Along Marinero, several rustic restaurants offer beach chairs and a place to pass the day while enjoying cool drinks and fresh seafood.

Puerto Angelito and **Playa Manzanillo** share the same sheltered cove, but are separated by a rocky outcropping. Located just west of town, they are accessible by walking from town along a dirt road, or by a launch taxi boat from the main beach. Here, the surf subsides enough for comfortable swimming, and hammock and palapa shade rentals are available. This is Puerto Escondido's best spot for snorkeling.

The main street for dining and nightlife is the one fronting Zicatela beach, Avenida del Morro. Increasingly, attention is turning to this area, where there are clean, inexpensive bungalow-style hotels, cafés that feature cheap, surfer-size breakfasts, cyber-stations for checking e-mail, and abundant beach bars with extended happy hours.

Recently, there is more of a health-conscious air to Puerto, with yoga classes, vegetarian meals, and book exchanges gaining in popularity, with herbal tea and espresso drinks becoming almost as ubiquitous as cold *cervezas.* During the winter months, Puerto is also noted for its excellent live music scene, though it depends in part on who happens to be in town at the time.

Concerns about safety have led civic leaders to place lifeguard stations along the main beaches and install nighttime lighting.

You can fly in from Mexico City or Oaxaca, drive, or take a bus along the scenic Mexican 175 highway through the mountains from Oaxaca. It's only 250 km (155 miles) but takes a full day. You can also arrive by taxi or car from Huatulco, which takes just about two hours along a fairly well-maintained two-lane highway.

DAY TRIPS FROM PUERTO ESCONDIDO

The diverse geography surrounding Puerto Escondido is complemented by a collection of small coastal towns, making it an ideal place from which to explore some uniquely Mexican cultural experiences.

The Southern Coast to Puerto Angel

The beaches south of Puerto Escondido are prime nesting grounds for the endangered **Ridley sea turtles.** During the summer months, visitors to this area may encounter turtles laying their eggs in the sand, or hatchlings making their first instinctive voyage to sea. The **Centro Mexicano la Tortuga** aquarium and research center was established by the Mexican government in 1991, in the beach village of **Mazunte.** Located about 72 km (45 miles) south of Puerto Escondido, (take the clearly marked turnoff to Puerto Angel from Mex. 200 south) it showcases the various species of turtles found along Mexican beaches, and is involved in efforts along this coast to protect the turtle nests.

This coast also has a succession of truly idyllic beaches, wide open and wild—but be aware that the currents here are extremely strong, and swimming is not recommended. However, enjoying a lunch of fresh fish, followed by a *siesta* in a hammock strung between two palms makes the trip absolutely worthwhile. The loveliest beach is **San Agustinillo;** the most renown is **Zipolite,** for its acceptance of nude sunbathing. Though Mexican law prohibits nudity of any kind on its beaches, custom dictates a spirit of tolerance here. As a result, the small town at this beach attracts free spirits to its inventive collection of budget accommodations — often consisting of little more than sleeping hammocks.

An additional 8 km (5 miles) down the coast road from Mazunte is the dusty beach village **Puerto Angel,** once considered a prime destination for backpackers and budget travelers. This place truly is a "sleepy little fishing village," though a succession of natural disasters (hurricane and earthquake damage in the past four years) have made it less desirable for long-term stays. In addition, the Naval Base is what now dominates the once picturesque central town beach. The best place to spend some relaxation time is at one of the beachfront restaurants at **Playa Panteón,** the lively cove located in front of the town cemetery (*panteón* means "cemetery").

Outdoor adventures can be exhausting, so feel free to fill-up on local fare at one of many food stands lining the beach.

Nearby Lagoons and Natural Attractions

The beaches to the north and south of Puerto Escondido are interspersed with lagoons, estuaries, and mangrove swamps, which contribute to making this region a fertile ecological paradise. About 24 km (15 miles) west of Puerto Escondido is **Laguna Manialtepec**, a deep lagoon, thick with vegetation and brimming with tropical birds, including the ibis, a variety of herons, parrots, egrets, and several species of ducks.

The 50-square mile national park, **Lagunas de Chacahua** is located 66 km (41 miles) to the north of Puerto Escondido. It is comprised of 32 km (20 miles) of fine, sandy beaches, backed by a pair of lagoons and jungle mangroves teeming with a changing array of tropical and migratory birds. Though crocodiles were hunted out in the 1970s, a crocodile hatchery in the village of Chacahua, located on the western edge of the lagoon, is steadily bringing them back.

Another neighboring venue for birdwatching is **Ventanilla Estuary,** where iguanas and crocodiles can be viewed in their natural habitat. Iguanas can also be seen at the nearby El Potrero iguana ranch.

Heading into the foothills of the Sierra de Miahuatlán, located north of Puerto Escondido, are numerous trails for hiking or horseback riding. This mountainous jungle region also features a few places of particular interest, including the **Atotonilco hot springs,** considered to be healing waters by the indigenous Chatino residents of the area. The **El Macuil waterfall** is not only a spectacular site, but offers cool, natural freshwater pools for swimming. Another waterfall can be enjoyed near the mountain village of **San Gabriel Mixtepec,** a small town nestled between several coffee plan-

Why not take a piece of Mexico home with you?
Enjoy a wide selection of local crafts in Huatalco.

tations. Nearby, the Mixtec village of **Jamiltepec** offers a
rare look at a quiet, traditional, indigenous town.

HUATULCO

Mexico's newest planned "resort," the Bays of Huatulco, is
still evolving, but has become known as the most eco-sensitive
resort along Mexico's Pacific coast. It is best known for its
series of exquisite, protected, pristine bays. Diving, snorkeling, bay cruises, and other water-oriented activities are the
main attractions here; dining, nightlife, and shopping remain
very limited.

It's biggest draw are the 36 beaches spread across the 35
km (22 miles) of coastline and nine bays, most of them still
undeveloped. The fact that the area has been slow to catch on
has resulted in a curious mix of ultra-modern infrastructure,
and unspoiled natural areas. Huatulco has what it takes to

attract visitors—including golf, tennis, water sports, fishing, a few restaurants and night spots, luxury accommodations, and direct flights from selected US cities—but hasn't developed its own distinct personality yet. For now, Huatulco is ideal for those who want to enjoy the beauty of nature during the day, then retreat to the well-appointed comfort of a luxury hotel by night.

The developed areas are easily divided into three sections: the original resort development at **Bahía Santa Cruz, Tangolunda Bay,** and the town of **Crucecita,** home to the area's residents and workers. The original settlement in this area is **Santa María de Huatulco,** a more traditional town found 17 miles inland approaching the Sierra foothills, but generally not explored by visitors to Huatulco.

Along with several older hotels, banks, and various tourist services, the Bahía Santa Cruz is home to a **marina,**

If you're feeling a bit adventurous, what better way to skim Santa Cruz Bay than atop a speeding jet ski?

from which numerous bay cruises and private *panga* fishing and sightseeing charters depart. Several seafood restaurants are located on a stretch of sheltered beach here, next to the marina. They double as daytime beach clubs, and have water-sports equipment for rent, along with food and beverage service. Adjacent to the marina is the "town's" central plaza, where the traditional central kiosk has been converted into a small stand selling espresso drinks, whole-bean coffee from the region, and tours to the neighboring coffee plantations — all sponsored by the coffee-growers' co-op. A small **artisan's market** separates the plaza from the main road, calle Juárez.

Crucecita is the true soul of this area, where all the shops, services, and facilities that make a town run are located. Recently, a few stylish, yet inexpensive, hotels have cropped up. The central plaza here is lovely and tree-lined, with a bandstand at its center. It fronts the **Iglesia Guadalupana,** the main church in town, which is decorated with an enormous ceiling mural of the Virgin of Guadalupe, set in a background of indigo-blue night sky; additional, brilliantly colored murals adorn the walls.

Tangolunda Bay is where the larger hotel developments are located, along with the 18-hole **Tangolunda Golf Course.**

Chahúe Bay lies between Tangolunda and Santa Cruz bays, and is the next to be slated for development. For now, it is home to a few beach clubs used by non-oceanfront hotels, and a small marina that is under construction. **Bahía Conejos** lies to the east of Tangolunda, and has residential developments already in progress.

Outlying Bays

Most people choose to visit the various outlying bays on an excursion boat. You can also charter a *panga* to drop you off, and arrange a return pick-up. The twin bays of **Maguey and El Órgano** are the closest and most popular, with a string of palapa restaurants and vendors who rent snorkeling gear and kayaks at Maguey.

Beyond these two bays, the landscape has more of a desert-like appearance, with large cacti interspersed among the palms. The bays of **Cacaluta, Chachacual,** and **Riscalillo** are still pristine and peaceful, with overnight camping allowed at Cacaluta. An exquisite beach is nestled into the cove of **Bahía San Agustín**, a small fisherman's village located about an hour by boat west of Santa Cruz, also accessible by road. Known for its outstanding offshore coral reefs, it's the favorite with divers and snorkelers.

DAY TRIPS FROM HUATULCO

The mountainous region north of Huatulco is considered a prime area for the production of *pluma* coffee, a Mexican coffee noted for its powerful aroma and rich, earthy flavor. Visits to the various **coffee *fincas*** (plantations), located just under two hours north of Crucecita by car, make for an interesting day or overnight trip. The production zone for Huatulco's coffee is comprised of over 50,000 hectares (100,000 acres), in the small towns surrounding the Copalita River. Notable are the continued use of traditional cultivation methods with minimal use of agricultural chemicals, and the open-air drying of the beans in sun beds.

The mountain areas surrounding the Capalita River are also the site of many natural treasures, including the **Capalitilla Cascades.** About 30 km (18.5 miles) north of Tangolunda a grouping of waterfalls, with heights averaging 25 m (80 feet) form natural Jacuzzis and clear pools for swimming. The area is also popular for horseback riding and rappelling.

Museums and Attractions

Casa Humbolt/Museo de Arte Virreinal. Calle Juan Ruíz de Alarcón 12, Taxco; Tel. (7) 622 5501. Tues–Sat 10am–6pm, Sun 10am–3pm. Admission 15 pesos.

Centro Internacional de Convivencia Infantil (CICI). Costera Miguel Alemán s/n and Cristobal Colón, Fracc Costa Azul, Acapulco; Tel. (7) 484 8210. Daily 10am–6pm. Admission 50 pesos.

Fuerte de San Diego. Costera Miguel Alemán, near the Zócalo, Acapulco; Tel. (7) 482 3828. Tues–Sun 10am–4:30pm.

Iglesia de Guadalupe. Calle Hidalgo 370, Puerto Vallarta; Tel. (3) 222-1326. Daily 7am–9pm. Admission free.

Iglesia Guadalupana. Central Park of La Crucecita, Huatulco. Daily 7am–9pm. Admission free.

La Quebrada. Acapulco. Daily noon–1pm and 7pm–10pm. Admission 15 pesos.

Mágico Mundo Marino. Islote Caleta and Caletilla, Acapulco; Tel. (7) 483 9344. Daily 9am–6pm. Admission 30 pesos.

Museo Universitario de Arqueología de Manzanillo. Glorieta de San Pedrito s/n, Manzanillo; Tel. (3) 332 2256. Tues–Sat 10am–2pm, 5pm–8pm, Sunday 10am–1pm. Admission 10 pesos, Sun free.

Museo Arqueológico de la Costa Grande. Agustín Ramírez and Paseo del Pescador, Zihuatanejo. Tues–Sun 10am–6pm. Admission 10 pesos.

Museo de la Platería. Plaza Borda 1, Taxco; No Phone. Daily 10am–5pm. Admission 15 pesos.

Museo de Taxco Guillermo Spratling. Plazuela Profesor Porfirio A. Delgado #1, Taxco; Tel. (7) 622 1660. Tues–Sun 9am–6pm. Admission 20 pesos, Sun and holidays free.

Museo Río Cuale. Isla Rio Cuale s/n (below lower bridge), Puerto Vallarta; No phone. Mon–Sat 10am–2pm. Donation of 5 pesos suggested.

WHAT TO DO

Spend any time in this area, and you'll quickly realize that life along Pacific Mexico is much more than "just a beach." There is a wealth of outdoor adventures, cultural encounters, and the simple pleasures of local village life .

ENTERTAINMENT

Fiestas

Mexico is known for its countless festivities and perennial spirit of celebration—Mexicans may have even invented the "art of the party." In Mexico, it's a given that any reason is a reason to celebrate, and traditional *fiestas* will include the entire family, with plenty of food and drink, contributed by all those involved.

Mexico's folkloric traditions have become the centerpiece of the modern **"Mexican Fiesta,"** created especially with the tourist in mind. These full evenings of entertainment generally include a makeshift marketplace featuring artesanía for sale, a buffet Mexican dinner, games (involving drinking large quantities of tequila), mariachi music, a presentation of folkloric dance from around the country, and a generous supply of margaritas and other beverages. Most of the time these are smallish presentations, with dances performed by amateur groups; at their worst, they can be truly gaudy and almost laughable shows.

The exception is in Acapulco. The Centro de Convenciones offers arguably the best Fiesta Mexicana in the country, and is the closest you'll come to an authentic display of Mexican culture and dance. Along with beautifully performed folkloric dances from all over Mexico, you'll witness a pre-Hispanic ceremony called *Los Voladores de Papantla*, which represents an invocation to the four cardinal points and a prayer for fertility; a *floreador* roping exhibition; and the vibrant sounds of the mariachi. This fiesta is held every Monday, Wednesday, and Friday from 7 to 10pm. Reservations are recommended, to ensure a good table. For reservations, call Tel. (7) 484-7046.

In Puerto Vallarta one fiesta that stands out from the rest is not a traditional Fiesta Mexicana at all, but an evening at the secluded Caletas cove, accessible only by boat. *Ritmos de la Noche* ("Rhythms of the Night") is a truly magical experience. You travel by fast catamarans to the former home of John Huston, where you'll be greeted by native drums and abundant tiki torches—there is no electricity here—then dine by candlelight at tables set along the secluded beach. Following dinner, the jungle, sounds of nature, and a replica of a pyramid are the backdrop for a performance of pre-Hispanic dances with

a unique contemporary choreographic twist. The show is held from Monday through Saturday. Call Tel. (3) 221-0657, for reservations.

Nightlife

Any place built on pleasing vacationers is bound to have its share of nocturnal attractions. Along Pacific Mexico, the options are as varied as the towns themselves, rang-

Vallarta's malecón is the perfect place to catch a traditional performance.

Burning the midnight oil... Step out for a night out on the town at one of Acapulco's many beachside bars.

ing from the dazzling discos of Acapulco to the quaint week-ly "dances" on dirt floors in Barra de Navidad.

Puerto Vallarta is making a name for itself with its vast selection of live music. One stretch of street—Ignacio L. Vallarta, just across the southbound bridge—is known as Rockin' Row, for its eclectic collection of clubs. Within easy walking distance from one another, you'll find a blues club, a Harley-Davidson-theme rock n' roll club, a salsa dance club, live mariachi music, a glitzy gay club (with nightly leather ranch-hands' show), an alternative dance club, and a sports bar.

Still, the malecón rules when it comes to sheer rowdy nighttime fun. Along with the longstanding Carlos O'Brians, several open-air bars and dance clubs stay open until 5am, and a new Cuban restaurant-bar pleases patrons with authentic food and live music nightly until 3am. Just a few blocks in back of the malecón are a growing collection of unique clubs with a more urban edge. Among them is La Cantina, a hipper version of a Mexican classic. By day it serves classic cantina fare, by night it clamors with the sound of conversation mixed with the best in contemporary recorded Mexican music. Board games are available for play.

Marina Vallarta is quieter at night, with the lighthouse-top lounge, El Faro, a favorite for spending a romantic evening, listening to live flamenco guitar. Along the Hotel Zone, the throwback disco Christine still manages to draw a crowd for the nightly midnight laser show, and J&B is a very hot spot for true Latin dancing; a

> **Local bullfights along the Pacific Coast are not up to standard—for a true experience of a *corrida de toros*, go to the *Plaza México* in Mexico City.**

favorite with locals, it's open until 5am. Also downtown, you'll find the imported Hard Rock Café, Planet Hollywood, and Hooters, but they tend to draw lesser crowds than the locally-owned options.

You'll find a more traditional nightlife, consisting of a weekly "dance" that takes place in an outdoor stadium or on a makeshift dance floor in smaller coastal towns such as Yelapa, Cruz de Loreto, and Barra de Navidad. Banda or ranchero-style music tends to dominate, but anything from hip-hop to classic rock may be tossed in for good measure.

Manzanillo, Ixtapa, and Zihuatanejo offer less in the way of nightlife. Manzanillo's clubs are few, but crowded, and feature recorded music for dancing. The Latin music clubs get going around 10pm, and don't even show up before midnight at the techno and alternative clubs. The majority of clubs, and the ubiquitous Carlos 'n' Charlie's, are located along the main boulevard, Miguel de la Madrid. In Ixtapa, sunset happy hours offer the most options, and Mexican fiestas seem to be a "best bet" for a complete evening. Other later night offerings are a sampling of what you'll find in any resort town in Mexico: Christine's disco at the Krystal Hotel, Sr. Frogs, and Carlos 'n' Charlie's. The only really original option here is the club, La Valentina, a combination restaurant/video bar with a desert-inspired décor.

There is no doubt that Acapulco rules when it comes to nightlife. In fact, I would venture that most visitors here come especially for that. Anyone that believes disco is dead hasn't been to Acapulco—it's alive and well, and happens nightly in an array of clubs that get going around midnight and often close after the sun comes up. The most majestic of these, Enigma, Palladium, and Fantasy, are located in the Las Brisas section of town, with towering, floor-to-ceiling windows overlooking stunning views of Acapulco Bay in all its night-lit splendor.

Along the main Hotel Zone, clubs are closed-in, but still offer sultry-hot music made for dancing; among them are Alebriges, Andromeda, and Baby-O. The Condessa stretch of the Costera is host to a string of open-air beach bars, with the most popular being Disco Beach, El Sombrero, and the pirate-theme Barbaroja. These offer dancing under the stars with a view of the ocean. The crowd here is young—very young—and the general rule is that one cover charge entitles you to all you can drink. Special coupons are handed out aggressively on the beaches during the day, in hopes of luring the biggest crowd that night.

If Acapulco's legendary fame reached its zenith in the 1940s and 1950s, why not visit a legend of a nightspot? The photos on the walls of Pepe's Piano Bar attest to the fact it has hosted more stars than the Acapulco sky—many of whom have joined in to entertain the audience in this red-velvet enclave of lounge music and martinis. Another exclusively Acapulco night spot is Salon Q, located across from the Convention Center. This Latin dance club features live shows each weekend with impersonators doing their best on the hottest talents of the day. Tequilas Le Club, located in the old section of town, is a long-standing Acapulco cabaret that offers two female impersonator shows nightly—one "international" version, with the later show featuring Latin divas.

SPORTS AND OUTDOOR ACTIVITIES

Although this region originally attracted the attention of visitors due its spectacular beaches backed by tropical jungle landscapes, Pacific Mexico also offers a varied geography tailor-made for sports and outdoor activities. The temperate, tropical climate means you are likely to enjoy sunshine throughout the year, and only seasonal, late afternoon rains in the summer months might interrupt a golf game or other active endeavor. Of particular interest are the increasing variety of ecologically and culturally oriented tours and excursions now available here.

If you enjoy golf, then search no further—Golfers will be amazed at the shortage of crowds and reasonable prices.

Active Sports

Golf and Tennis

Golf. The area from Punta Mita on the northern tip of Banderas Bay to Manzanillo in the south is beginning to rival Los Cabos as Mexico's golf mecca. Six exceptional golf courses are located here, notable not only for their challenging designs coupled, with ocean and jungle views, but also for their absence of crowds and reasonable prices. The newest is the Jack Nicklaus–designed course at the Four Seasons Punta Mita (Tel. (3) 291-6000) located 30 minutes north of Puerto Vallarta, notable for a spectacular hole that drives to a natural island 175 yards offshore. Currently, it is open only to guests of the Four Seasons, or members of other golf clubs with a letter of introduction. Two other courses are located near Puerto Vallarta: Club de Golf Flamingos (Tel. (3) 298-0606), a casual course open to the public, and the Joe Finger–designed course at the Marina Vallarta Golf Club (Tel. (3) 221-0073). Four new courses are scheduled to open in the surrounding area by mid 2001.

Traveling south along the Costa Alegre, two spectacular courses offer exclusive play and multiple ocean views. Isla Navidad (Tel. (3) 355-5103) is one of Mexico's top-rated resort courses, designed by Robert Von Hagge. It features wide-open fairways and big greens, with plenty of water, including eight oceanside holes. The course at El Tamarindo (Tel. (3) 551-5031) may not be as renown as the others, but it is a lush beauty of a course set in a tropical rainforest by the sea. The approaches to the holes wind through jungle paths, and fairways and greens are gently worked into the mountainous terrain bordering the Pacific Ocean.

In Manzanillo, golf is an integral part of the Las Hadas resort where La Mantarray golf course (Tel. (3) 334-0000), designed by Roy and Pete Dye, is considered among the most scenic in the world. Compact and challenging, 12 of the 18 holes are played over water, including its signature 18th hole, with a drive to an island green.

Further south, Ixtapa has two solid courses: the Robert Trent Jones Jr.–designed Club de Golf Ixtapa Palma Real (Tel. (7) 553-1062), and the more challenging Club de Gold Marina Ixtapa (Tel. (7) 553-1410), designed by Robert Von Hagge.

Acapulco also offers two golf courses: the Acapulco Princess Golf Course (Tel. (7) 469-1000), known for its several water hazards, and designed by Ted Robinson, and the Club de Golf Acapulco (Tel. (7) 484-0781), a popular public course located across from the El Cano hotel.

The southernmost golf course is the 18-hole, par 72, Tangolunda Golf Course (Tel. (9) 58 1-0037) in Huatulco. It's a rather small and narrow course, designed by Mario Schjetnan Dantán.

Green fees range between US$55 and US$135. Most golf courses have carts and clubs for rent.

Tennis. Courts are so plentiful, you rarely have to wait to play. All destinations discussed in this book have courts in excellent condition at the higher end hotels, with some offering lighted or covered play, and a range of surfaces. The best tennis facilities are in Puerto Vallarta, where the tennis-aficionado will find two top-class tennis centers. The Continental Plaza Tennis Club, located in the Hotel Continental Plaza (Tel. (3) 224-0123 ext. 500), offers eight courts, open for play daily from 7am until 10pm. The Iguana Tennis Center (Tel. (3) 221-0683), located just off the highway near the entrance to Marina Vallarta, has three courts, one outdoor and two covered, with astro-turf surfaces. Court fees range between US$8 and US$20 per hour. Most tennis courts and many hotels offer racket rentals ranging between US$3 and US$6 per day.

Water Sports

Puerto Vallarta and Banderas Bay have some of the most dramatic **diving and snorkeling** along the Mexican Pacific Coast. The enormous bay offers sheltered waters that are inhabited by myriad marine creatures. Among the amazing sea life are the giant mantas and eagle mantas that traverse the bay. Dives in the shallower parts of the bay allow a close-up look at thousands of types of tropical fish, including several species endemic to the bay's waters. Night dives are particularly exciting, offering a chance to discover the thriving nocturnal habitat of Los Arcos, the imposing rock formation that juts out of the southern shore of the bay. Two of the best-reputed dive shops in Vallarta are Vallarta Adventures in Marina Vallarta (Tel. (3) 221-0657) and Chico's Dive Shop (Tel. (3) 222-1895). Dive rates in Vallarta range between US$60 and US$120 for a two-tank dive. Quimixto Coves and Los Arcos are the most locally popular dive spots; exceptional diving farther out includes the underwater grottos at the Islas Marietas, and offshore at La Corbeteña.

Every cove along the coast from Puerto Vallarta south to Huatulco has the potential to be a great **snorkeling** spot. Isla Ixtapa in Ixtapa, and the numerous coves and islets around Huatulco are prime spots, with calm waters for beginners. Most bay cruises offer snorkeling as part of their excursion. Also, dive shops and most of the larger, beachfront hotels rent snorkeling gear, so you can explore the beaches on your own. Whenever you visit a beach that faces the open sea remember to exercise caution—check with the locals as to whether or not the beaches are safe for swimming.

Deep-sea fishing is excellent all along the Pacific coast. Manzanillo has earned a reputation for being one of the best year-round spots for marlin and sailfish. Winter is best for dorado (also known as *mahi-mahi*), and in summer wahoo and roosterfish are the main catches. The premier season is from October through February and rates range from US$180 to US$350 for a private fishing charter. Fishing can be arranged through travel agencies or directly at the fishermen's cooperative (Tel. (3) 332-1031), located downtown where the fishing boats are moored.

As **sea kayaking** continues to grow in popularity, more venues are making it available along Mexico's Pacific. Many of the eco-conscious tour operators offer sea kayaking expeditions, as do a growing number of upscale hotels. In Puerto Vallarta, contact Open Air Expeditions (Tel. (3) 222-3310) for tours guided by professionals. In Huatulco, Shuatur (Tel. (9) 587-0734) and Turismo Conejo (Tel. (9) 587-0029) are well equipped to arrange excellent sea-kayaking adventures. It is easy to find operators offering **water-skis, windsurfing boards, parasailing,** and noisy little **wave-runners** for rent by the hour on the beaches of most hotels.

Puerto Escondido's Zicatela Beach is considered one of the best **surfing** beaches in the world, and is the site of an important surfing competition every August. San Blas, located 225 km (150 miles) northwest of Puerto Vallarta, is another good spot for outstanding surfing waves. The

Lookout for that pigeon! Sail into the sky for a bird's-eye view of Puerto Vallarta.

best waves along the Mexican coast are caught during the fall. San Blas has a much smaller tourist infrastructure than Puerto Escondido, and word-of-mouth is the best way to learn the secrets of the best beaches and current breaks. Another good option is to contact Surf-Mex (Tel. (3) 223-1680), based in Puerto Vallarta, who offer surf tours and lessons, from rank beginners on up to expert wave-riders.

Excursions & Eco-tours

Eco- and adventure-tourism fans will feel they've reached nirvana here. With an increasing number of tourists looking for these options, the Mexican Association of Adventure Travel and Eco-tourism (AMTAVE; Tel. (5) 663-5381, or www.amtave.com.mx) was formed to offer information about the most qualified guides and authentic service providers in each area of Mexico, and can direct you to qualified members in the area.

A word for those enamored of **hiking:** As a rule, in Mexico there are no marked trails or ranger stations such as you commonly find in the US and Europe. Therefore, it is better to go with a local operator or qualified guide, or contact a company in the US or Europe that can arrange something that fits your ability and sense of adventure. The Sierra Madre Mountains adjacent to Puerto Vallarta offer challenging, yet accessible hiking and mountain biking. Bike-Mex (Tel. (3) 223-1834) offers expert guided tours into the mountains and other outlying areas as well as **mountain biking** expeditions to challenge every rider's skill level.

Whether along a deserted stretch of beach, or in the foothills of tropical mountains, **horseback riding** is an excellent way to enjoy the exquisite landscapes of Pacific Mexico. Tour operators and travel agencies in all the destinations listed in this guide can arrange horseback tours, or you may even be approached by independent operators while you sunbathe at the beach. In Puerto Vallarta you will find some of the finer ranches with well-cared for horses (the ones at the beaches are apt to be scrawny). These ranches offer daytime or sunset rides into the Sierra Madre mountains for both experienced and inexperienced riders. One particularly outstanding operation is Rancho Palma Real, which offers a long four- to six-hour ride into the fertile valley that extends from the foothills of the Sierra Madre, along a river and up to an absolutely beautiful waterfall.

Huatulco has turned into somewhat of a haven for travelers looking for activities that not only put their physical fitness to the test but also offer an intense communion with nature. Outstanding **river kayaking** and **river rafting** trips take place along the Zimatán and Copatita rivers, with descents from class I to IV. The excitement of the trip is surpassed only by the breathtaking, panoramic views. Huatulco is also the place for **rappelling** with descents over Punta Celeste, Piedra de Moros, and the Copalitilla waterfalls. For details on the qualified companies offering these and other outdoor activities, contact the Huatulco Visitors Bureau (Tel. (9) 587-1037).

Manzanillo and Puerto Vallarta are both noted for **birdwatching.** Manzanillo's best birdwatching takes place in the several lagoons that lie along the coastline, especially Laguna de las Garzas, (also know as Laguna de San Pedrito), and Laguna de Cuyutlán—both near the downtown and hotel zones. Both are notable for the variety of species and the abundance of herons and white pelicans. Puerto Vallarta offers several options in surrounding areas, so birdwatchers can opt for mountain or coastal experiences. Nearby is one of the top birdwatching lagoons in America, the Laguna del Quelele. The offshore Marietas Islands offer the rare opportunity to sight Blue- (and Yellow-) Footed Booby Birds. Open Air Expeditions (Tel. (3) 222-3310), offers some of the better-organized tours led by expert guides.

Located 150 miles north of Vallarta is the small coastal town of **San Blas,** once an important port, but now primarily noted for its abundant birds. The best sightings are along the Tovara River, up to the La Tovava natural springs. Jungle cruises in small boats can be arranged through the Hotel Garza Canela in San Blas (Tel. (3) 285-0307), or through any Puerto Vallarta travel agency. In Zihuatanejo, local travel agencies can arrange for day trips to Los Morros de los Pericos island, where a great variety of birds nest.

Whale-watching is an awe-inspiring experience, and the Mexican Pacific is one of the few places in the world that offers an opportunity to view these majestic mammals in their natural habitat. From late November through March, the waters of Banderas Bay become the breeding and calving grounds for hundreds of migrating humpback whales,

Whale-watching in Puerto Vallarta — there's no secret why colonial Spaniards once called this area "Humpback Bay."

much to the delight of the hundreds of visitors that enjoy witnessing the breaching, spy-hopping, leaps, and other displays of whale behavior. Eco-conscious tour operators throughout the bay (most are based in Puerto Vallarta) have voluntarily established norms for whale-watching, which allow up-close observation while disturbing them as minimally as possible. Authorized and knowledgeable tour operators include Vallarta Adventure (Tel. (3) 221-0657), and Open Air Expeditions (Tel. (3) 222-3310). Whales have even been known to swim right alongside Puerto Vallarta's main boardwalk, the malecón, giving its visitors a special treat.

Another seasonal, and very worthwhile eco-conscious activity, is to participate in the nightly **sea turtle releases and watches** that take place from August through November along the shores of Banderas Bay, and further south in Mazunte (located between Huatulco and Puerto Escondido). Preservation groups and trained specialists conduct these releases and watches. You participate by helping to collect the turtles' eggs and taking them to a safe nesting area for incubation. After the baby turtles hatch, they are released back into the ocean. Organized visits to the turtle camps are conducted daily in Mazunte, at the Centro Mexicano de la Tortuga, and in Puerto Vallarta by several of the beachfront hotels and a select group of ecologically oriented tour operators, such as Eco-tours de México (Tel. (3) 222-6606).

When it comes to unforgettable experiences, few compare to the unique feeling of **swimming with dolphins,** and Mexico has some of the best dolphin centers in the world. Dolphin Adventure in Puerto Vallarta is considered the best in Latin America, both for its exceptional treatment of these mammals as well as its affiliated research and environmental education programs. This interactive dolphin center offers a free-form swim with the dolphins, with a strictly limited number of participants, as well as a "Dolphin Encounter," where they learn about these mammals in an up-close and personal manner. Acapulco has two dolphin centers, CICI (Centro Internacional de Convivencia Infantil) located across from the Convention Center, and at Paradise on La Condesa beach. These centers are more for show and entertainment than for true research and education. Prices for these dolphin experiences vary between US$65 and US$160.

Guided Tours

City Tours of both Puerto Vallarta and Manzanillo are offered by virtually every local tour operator. **Bay Tours** are very popular in every coastal destination from Puerto Vallarta down to Huatulco, and are also an excellent way to get your bearings, from the vantage point of the waters off-shore. In Puerto Vallarta, a cruise may be on any type vessel, from a charter sailboat to an oversize catamaran, even to an exact replica of Christopher Columbus's *Santa Maria*. There is something to fit every taste. Both day and sunset cruises are offered; day cruises generally include visits to funky or secluded beaches that are only accessible by boat. In Acapulco the *Yate Fiesta* and the *Aca Tiki* are the long-running favorites for sunset cocktail cruises..

Another specialty of Acapulco are the glass-bottom boat tours to La Roqueta, where for US$4 you can view something unique and characteristic of Mexico's spirit—an underwater statue of the *Virgen de Guadalupe*. In Zihuatanejo, an elegant trimaran glides along the small bay for a memorable sunset cruise. In Huatulco a tour of the nine bays is a considered a "must" to truly experience the place; you can hire a panga from the well-organized fisherman's cooperative or join one of the organized tours offered by several local tour operators. Both depart from the marina in Santa Cruz.

ATV **Jungle Tours** are a fun, albeit rowdier way to see the off-the-beaten-path areas surrounding Puerto Vallarta and Huatulco. For details in Huatulco contact Cantera Tours (Tel. (9) 581-0030); in Puerto Vallarta call Pathfinders at Chico's Dive Shop (Tel. (3) 222-1875). If you like the adventure of traveling through the jungle, Vallarta Adventure in Puerto Vallarta, offers an extraordinary tour of the Sierra Madre Mountains on board Mercedes Benz all-terrain vehicles (called *Unimogs*). The tour includes a visit to a secluded beach and a detailed explanation of the flora and fauna of the area.

La Quebrada cliff-divers prepare for a death-defying plunge into the waters below.

Lovers of speed and thrill-seekers will enjoy the fast-paced tour along the Papagayo River, 72 km (48 miles) north of Acapulco. Shotover-Jet (Tel. (7) 484-1154), travels aboard specially-designed 12-passenger turbo boats, which come screaming up to the face of the canyon, and then make a fast spin before continuing up the river, while making repeated 360° turns. To say that it's a rush is an understatement, and their eco-conscious pamphlet is good for a chuckle, considering the reality of the experience. They are, however, making new rafting excursions available for those who prefer to experience the Papagayo River a little closer to its natural state.

Spectator Sports

If **cliff-diving** is a sport and not a form of insanity, Acapulco's **La Quebrada** cliff-divers have to be the champs. The sight is not to be believed—except that you absolutely must believe in the authenticity of their kneeling before a shrine to the Virgin of Guadalupe just before plunging head first into a narrow slit of water, 130 feet below. Performances are daily at 1pm, and each evening at 7:15, 8:15, 9:15, and 10:15pm, for roughly $1 US admission to the public viewing platform.

The lightning-fast Basque version of handball, **jai-alai,** is played in Acapulco at the Frontón, where tournaments attract numerous fans of the *peloteiros* as the players are called.

SHOPPING

At first glance, shopping in Pacific Mexico may seem disappointing. Take a closer look, however, and you'll find that a few key areas offer truly singular shopping opportunities, and a chance to experience a bit of Mexico's cultural soul in the process.

The larger beach destinations have all the requisite silver, souvenir, and T-shirt shops, plus a few worthwhile boutiques selling higher quality clothing. Basically, you'll find the same names in Acapulco, Puerto Vallarta, Ixtapa, and Huatulco.

Acapulco is the place for boutiques and designer clothing. It has no original works of *artesanía* of its own, but it still retains its historical identity as a trading port. You can find goods here from all over Mexico, including silver from nearby Taxco, Talavera pottery from Puebla, and Barro Negro, the shiny black ceramic from Oaxaca. Artesanía created closer to home, in Acapulco's home state of Guerrero, includes lacquered chests and plates from Olinalá, as well as the white *huipiles* (an indigenous style blouse), embroidered in brightly colored shades of orange, red, and *Rosa Mexicano* (hot pink). Other traditional Acapulco wares are coconut shell carvings, usually monkey's heads, as well as decorative seashell ornaments, and regional candies made of coconut and tamarind.

Puerto Vallarta has more to offer shoppers in search of creative *artesanía*. Vallarta is a great place to buy authentic—even custom-made huaraches (the flat-sole leather sandals)—as well as *manta* cotton clothing, often decorated with colorful hand-painted designs. Silver jewelry seems to be available everywhere, from the elegant shops along the malecón, to strolling beach vendors.

There are also several shops in Puerto Vallarta that offer exquisite home accessories, with a definite Mexican style to them. Talavera pottery and dishes, as well as blown-glass

In Puerto Vallarta, shoppers can find all types of artesanía ranging from silver jewelry to custom-made huaraches.

stemware in a rainbow of colors, are readily found throughout the Pacific coastal region.

Markets

Wherever you go, you'll find a market where artesanía of various types and quality are interspersed with local clothing, woven handbags, hippie-style jewelry, religious memorabilia, and regional foods. Acapulco and Puerto Vallarta also have flea markets, with stalls of souvenirs, T-shirts, huaraches, silver jewelry, wooden puppets, traditional Mexican rag dolls, onyx chess sets, ceramics, and other representative goods from around Mexico.

Best Buys

Ceramics. Both Talavera ceramics from Puebla, and majolica ceramics are found in the region—but don't mistake one for the other. Both have the same style, using bright colors like yellow, burnt orange, and royal blue, or a blue and off-white scheme, in designs that include flowers, birds and geometric shapes. The only way that you can tell them apart is by looking on the back of the piece and checking for the mark and the signature of the maker—only ceramics that have been handcrafted in Talavera, Puebla can be called "Talavera." All other ceramics with the same technique and design are known as "majolica." Because Talavera comes from

When buying jewelry or other items made of silver, be sure to look for the .925 stamp, which ensures the measure of the silver content of the piece. However, even if it is visible, be aware that most of the silver-colored jewelry sold by strolling beach venders is made from *alpaca*, a lesser quality metal with a heavy copper content. Established stores are your best bet for quality silver purchases.

84

a very specific region and only a few workshops produce this type of ceramic, it is more expensive than majolica, even though majolica can be just as beautiful.

Leather goods. Jalisco is especially noted for its tooled leather goods, an art stemming from the traditions of the *charros* (Mexican ranchers, highly skilled in the roping and handling of horses), dating back to the days of the *haciendas*. No self-respecting charro would be caught without his *cinturón piteado*, a tooled leather belt, decorated with *piteado*, a type of fine work where thin threads are sewn into the leather forming beautiful flower or geometric patterns that may even include the owner's name. This same workmanship may be appreciated in authentic charro boots and fine saddles. The finer the thread, and the more complex the pattern, the more expensive the piece.

Tequila and mezcal. What better place to get the real thing than a Mexican resort that just happens to be located in the state where all tequila is produced? Puerto Vallarta is located 330 km (205 miles) from the source of all production, the town of Tequila. A good bottle of tequila—made, bought, and sampled in Jalisco—has no match. Make certain to look for the Agave Azul (100% blue agave) legend on the bottle to ensure you are purchasing Tequila's best. One of the best paces to buy a bottle is the Casa del Tequila in downtown Puerto Vallarta. They regularly host samplings, serve up the best margaritas on the coast, and provide free informational pamphlets (in English and Spanish) on the history, types, and lore of tequila. (Also see page 93.)

In Puerto Escondido and Huatulco, you'll find an abundance of tequila's close cousin, mezcal. Mezcal is distilled from the juice of more common types of maguey plants found in the central region of Mexico. It has a stronger taste and smell than tequila. Oaxacan mezcal is the type that is

In search of original Huichol art? Then visit Puerto Vallarta —no town has a larger collection of this traditional art form.

bottled with a maguey worm pickled in the bottom of the bottle. To the ancient Mexicans, the maguey plant was considered sacred, and the fact that the worm had ingested a part of the "spirit" of this revered plant made consuming them both a delicacy and a way to obtain good luck. *Salud!*

Contemporary art. Puerto Vallarta offers a unique opportunity to view an excellent cross-section of Latin American art. Works by recognized masters—including contemporaries José Luis Cuevas and Alejandro Colunga—as well as emerging artists, are on display at the numerous art galleries in town. Notable among the galleries are Galería Pacífico (Tel. (3) 222-1982) and Galería Rosas Blanca (Tel. (3) 222-1168), located downtown; and Galería Flores and Arte de las Americas (Tel. (3) 221-1985), in Marina Vallarta. It is important to note that original art is duty free in the US and many European countries, and that most galleries are experts in packing, shipping, and handling.

During the winter months, the various galleries, that number more than a dozen, host free art walks. These events showcase featured artists' works, and are also an integral part of the local social scene.. The large presence of both galleries and artists have positioned Puerto Vallarta as a leading art center, the site of the largest selection of fine contemporary Mexican art outside of Mexico City.

Huichol art. You won't find any other town in Mexico with as much original Huichol art as Puerto Vallarta. The Huichol are one of the last remaining indigenous cultures that has been successful in retaining cultural integrity — despite efforts by the "civilized" world to westernize their traditional ways of living. Because their land, located in remote areas of the high Sierra Madre mountains, has diminished in productivity, they can no longer produce enough for self-sufficiency, and have been forced to look for supplemental forms of income. One of these is by selling their art.

Huichol art is vibrant, full of symbolism, and is generally created as a result of a spiritual "vision." There are two main forms of this art. Yarn paintings are created on a wooden base covered with wax; colorful threads are pressed into the wax to form designs that are symbolic representations of the world of the Huichol. Beaded pieces are made in the same manner, by pressing tiny beads into carved wooden pieces that are coated in wax. The designs are called *chaquira*, and their different animals and symbols give meaning to the piece.

You can also find Huichol ceremonial and everyday life artifacts for sale at galleries that specialize in Huichol. As a rule, none of the objects offered for sale — especially those deemed ceremonial, such as the Muvieris and Marakame hats and chairs—have been used in actual ceremonies. In the Huichol culture it is considered a sacrilege to commercialize sacred objects. Visitors should be aware of this and respect their culture by not attempting to purchase sacred or ceremonial pieces.

THE PACIFIC COAST FOR CHILDREN

Mexico is a country that welcomes children. You will find very few places that do not include some kind of family-oriented attraction. Puerto Vallarta, with its miles of beaches, is among the most appropriate resorts for families. Most four- and five-star hotels offer supervised "Kids Clubs" and organized children's activities for a nominal daily fee.

Children enjoy boat rides and bay cruises. The glass-bottom boat ride in Acapulco seems to be one that they find the most fun. Boat rides in Puerto Vallarta's Bay of Banderas include the added excitement of sighting dolphins, mantas, and, depending on the season, even whales.

Bargaining

Street, market, and beach vendors, as well as modest handicraft stands, are all prepared to bargain. Hotel gift shops, government handicraft outlets, department stores, and fine boutiques all have fixed prices. However, you shouldn't enter into the haggling game unless you are really ready to buy—and don't propose a price that is insultingly low. Begin by offering about 20 % less than you are willing to pay. A useful phrase is, "What's the lowest you'll go?" (¿Cuánto es lo menos?). You can always break off a deadlock in a pleasant way, saying "gracias," and indicating that you want to look around. If you prefer not to bargain, simply ask if there is a discount (¿Me hace una rebaja?). Rest assured that whatever you finally pay, the seller is making a profit, and you will probably have your bargain.

There are several **waterparks:** In Acapulco, the **CICI** (Centro Internacional de Convivencia Infantil), across from the Convention Center, offers hours of fun with waterslides, a water center for toddlers, a fresh-water pool with waves, plus a dolphin and seal show, all included in the entrance fee of around US$4. Another waterpark is located near Caleta beach, called **Mundo Mágico Marino.** It features water-slides, an aquarium, pools—one is a saltwater pool—and boat rides. **El Rey León,** located near Pie de la Cuesta, is a large family-style restaurant with shallow pools and water-slides for children, plus a miniature train.In Puerto Vallarta, the **Mayan Palace Waterpark** in Marina Vallarta has water-slides, a lazy-river, and a mini-waterpark for young children. Children ten and older will be both moved and amazed by swimming with the dolphins, experiences that are available both in Acapulco and Puerto Vallarta.

Acapulco's public park **Parque Papagayo** is a good option for a day away from the water. It has a small amuse-ment park, an aviary, a replica of one of Columbus's ships, and paddleboats for cruising the park's channels. Another favorite with the younger crowd is **Amazing World** in the Gran Plaza. Here for one admission fee, children can enjoy slides, chutes, tunnels, a ball-filled pool, and video games.

In Puerto Vallarta, **Isla del Río Cuale** (Rio Cuale Island) is a small park. Saturday mornings, children can participate in painting and clay modeling workshops, as well as cultural activities that might include folkloric dance, impromptu plays, or story readings. Bowling is also a popular pastime, and both Puerto Vallarta and Acapulco have good facilities. In Puerto Vallarta the **Collage-Emporium Entertainment Center** has a bowling alley, video game arcade, and a cafete-ria. In Acapulco, the bowling alley is in Plaza Bahía, where they also have a small go-kart track and a video-game arcade.

Calendar of Events

January 1 *New Year's Day*: National holiday with parades, religious observances, parties, and occasional fireworks.

January 6 *Día de Reyes (Epiphany Day)*: Children receive gifts to commemorate the gifts presented to the Christ Child by the three wise men. A *rosca de reyes*, a round cake decorated with candied seasonal fruits, is baked with a small doll.inside. Whoever gets the doll must give a party for all present on the *Día de la Candelaria*.

February 2 *Día de la Candelaria*: A mix of pre-Hispanic and European traditions marking the end of winter. Music, dances, processions, and other festivities, including the blessing of candles and seeds.

February *Carnaval*: Revelry preceding the beginning of Lent.

March 21 *Benito Juárez's birthday*: National holiday; birthday of one of Mexico's heroes.

March Spring Equinox: Festivals welcome spring in the fashion of the ancient Mexicans, with dances and prayers.

March/April *Holy Week*: All Mexico celebrates from *Domingo de Ramos* (Palm Sunday) through Easter Sunday. Mexico's vacation week.

May 1 *Día del Trabajo*: National holiday, with parades in memory of striking workers killed in the late 1800s, which brought about reforms that ensure workers' rights today.

May 5 *Cinco de Mayo*: Celebrates the defeat of the French at the Battle of Puebla by a small and poorly armed Mexican army.

May *Día de Corpus Christi*. Six weeks after Easter, children wear indigenous dress, and take small animals and seeds to the church to be blessed.

June 1 *Día de la Marina*: Navy day, with colorful sea-parades in Acapulco and Puerto Vallarta.

July *Festival de Santiago:* Charreadas, Mexican style rodeos, in the states of Jalisco and Guerrero.

August 15 *Asuncion de la Virgen María*: Celebrates the assumption of the Virgin Mary with processions, masses, music, and fireworks.

September 15–16 *Día de la Independencia*: National holiday celebrating Mexico's independence from Spain in 1810. On the night of the 15th, the president of Mexico and all governors and mayors throughout Mexico give the historical *grito*, or shout for independence, with which Miguel Hidalgo signaled the beginning of the fight for Independence.

October 12 *Día de la Raza:* National Holiday commemorating the arrival of Christopher Columbus; now with a pre-Hispanic emphasis as a form of protest against the Spanish Conquest.

November 1–2 *Día de Los Santos Inocentes and Día de Muertos*: All Saint's Day and Day of the Dead. See page 40.

November *Fiestas del Mar*: In Puerto Vallarta, a month-long celebration with art and cultural festivals, sports events, the Mexico Boat Show, and a gourmet dining festival.

November 20 *Día de la Revolución*: National Holiday; the beginning of the War of Revolution against the government of Porfirio Díaz in 1910, which gave birth to the Mexican Constitution in 1917.

December 12 *Día de la Virgen de Guadalupe*: Mexico's patron saint is honored with processions, street fairs, fireworks, and masses.

December 16–24 *Posadas*: The journey of Joseph and Mary to Bethlehem commemorated with *Pastorelas*, plays that depict the journey, the breaking of *piñatas*, and Christmas carols.

December 24–25 *Noche Buena and Navidad*: The traditional celebration takes place on Christmas Eve; families gather for a late dinner, followed by midnight mass.

EATING OUT

Mexican cuisine is one of the world's most varied and unusual, with flavors that are exclusive to this country. The basic ingredients of Mexican food date back to pre-Hispanic times: corn, beans, a wide variety of *chiles* (peppers), tomatoes, squash, and avocado.

Corn, when soaked with lime and ground, is turned into *masa*, a dough used to make *tortillas*, *sopes* (medium size circles with pinched edges filled with beans, chicken or some other kind of meat), or *gorditas*, thicker rounds that are stuffed with a filling, then deep-fried. Masa may also be whipped with lard or shortening, then rolled and stuffed with a sweet or savory filling, wrapped in corn or banana leaves, and steamed to create *tamales*.

Beans are cooked with few seasonings, to contrast with the spices in the other dishes, and served with the main course. In Mexican households once the pot of beans has been around for a couple of days, the beans are mashed and fried; these are called *frijoles refritos* (refried beans).

The wide variety of *chiles* used in Mexican cuisine is another distinguishing feature. These chiles are known by different names, depending on whether they are dry or fresh, as drying can completely change the character of a chile. A fresh *chile poblano* has a mild, tangy flavor—however, when dried it's known as *chile ancho*, which has a rich earthy taste. Some chiles are much hotter than others, with the heat being so overwhelming that you can taste little else, like *chile habanero* and *chile piquín*. A pepper that is very spicy but has a sweet undertone is *chile de arbol*, a dried pepper similar to the peppers used in Hunan cooking. The famous *jalapeño* acquires a smoky, spicy flavor when dried, then called *chipotle*. Widely used in Mexican cooking is the *serrano*, a small green pepper that is hot but much tastier that its close cousin, the jalapeño, for which it is often mistaken.

Meals and Traditional Foods

Breakfast

In Mexico the first meal of the day is called *desayuno*. Normally it consists of eggs, refried beans, fruit, and steaming coffee, with or without milk. Eggs many be prepared in a variety of ways, including *huevos rancheros*—fried on top of a corn tortilla and smothered in a mildly spicy red sauce—or

---

The Proper Way to Drink Tequila

The very best tequila—and the only kind any self-respecting Mexican *aficionado* would consider drinking—is made from 100% agave, or, even better, 100% blue agave. This legend on the bottle will ensure the quality of the product you're buying.

If you like the strong flavor and full potency of this legendary drink go for the "blanco" tequila, which will be a transparent liquid of the briefest distillation and the highest alcohol content. It will generally be the least expensive kind. If you prefer a smoother taste, try the "reposado," which, due to a minimum period of aging in oak caskets, takes on a light golden color. It is usually sold in a clear bottle, so that you can appreciate the color. The smoothest tequila is labeled añejo for its lengthier aging process, and usually comes in more refined bottles. This is considered the best—much like a fine cognac — and is also the most expensive tequila.

Note that a common misconception that tequila should be "slammed" or gulped couldn't be further from the truth. In Mexico, good tequila is sipped, as you would a good cognac or brandy. The shot glass, or *caballito* as it is traditionally called in Jalisco, is generally good for four or five sips.

huevos a la Mexicana— scrambled with chopped onions, tomatoes, and serrano or jalapeño peppers. Late risers will be served *almuerzo*, or brunch, which is a heavier meal. Popular choices include *chilaquiles*—tortilla strips that have been fried and then simmered in a spicy broth, served with or without chicken or eggs, and topped with fresh grated cheese, sliced onions, and cream—or *carne con chile* —chopped steak in a spicy tomato-chile sauce. In Puerto Vallarta, and throughout the state of Jalisco, a traditional almuerzo consists of *birria,*

Hungry? Try *pescado en vara asado* (grilled fish on a stick), a Vallarta beach specialty.

served either as a stew or as a filling for tacos. Real birria is made with goat, but nowadays beef is more commonly used. It's prepared in a spicy broth, and accompanied by a hot sauce made of chile guajillo and vinegar. Another traditional brunch dish is *menudo,* a thick soup made of cow's stomach (not tripe) prepared in either a *blanco* (white) or *rojo* (red) broth, and served with chopped onion, lime, ground oregano, and hot sauce to taste. In Acapulco and Zihuatanejo traditional brunch dishes consist of *tortas de relleno,* a baguette-style roll filled with baked pork that has been stuffed with vegetables. Visitors to Guerrero, the home state of Acapulco and Zihuatanejo, will also commonly find *tamales de elote* (corn tamales) served with cream, cheese, and a warm red sauce.

Lunch

The afternoon meal is known as *comida,* and in Mexico, is considered the principal meal of the day. During these hours, however, most travelers to the Pacific coast will be beachside, enjoying the sun and the surf. Nothing compares to the pleasure of eating fresh seafood under a palapa by the sea. Beach dining can last for as many hours as you decide to spend by the sea, and may consist

> One of the simple pleasures of Pacific Mexico is *licuado*, a drink made from fresh tropical fruit—banana, papaya, watermelon, mango, guayaba and other fruits—blended with ice and either milk or water. It makes a filling snack, or can accompany lighter lunches.

of a series of small plates of food, accompanied by cold *cervezas,* margaritas, or refreshing coconut juice served in its shell. Delicacies enjoyed seaside are similar all along the coast. Most popular are fresh shrimp, lobster, or fish—look for *huachinango* (red snapper) and *dorado* (mahi-mahi), prepared either grilled with butter or *al mojo de ajo* (with garlic).

The regional fish specialty in Acapulco and Zihuatanejo is *pescado en talla,* a whole fish split in half and slowly cooked over a wood fire and seasoned with garlic, chopped tomatoes and onions, vinegar, and oregano. In Puerto Vallarta, *pescado sarandeado* is the regional specialty: a whole fish prepared in a marinade of soy sauce, orange juice, and spices, also cooked slowly over a wood fire. In Zihuatanejo, lobster tacos are very popular, as are *tiritas de pescado,* thin strips of fish marinated briefly in lime and orange juice, then served topped with finely chopped onions and serrano peppers. In Acapulco, *ceviche acapulqueño* is also a favorite, consisting of cubed fish marinated in lime juice and vinegar, served in a sauce of catsup, orange juice, and hot sauce with chopped onions and lime. Ceviche in Puerto Vallarta is very finely chopped fish, marinated in lime and mixed with grated carrot and cucumber, then served on *tostadas*, baked or fried tortillas. A true Vallarta beach specialty, sold by strolling vendors, is *pescado en vara asado,* a whole grilled fish on a stick.

If you prefer to have lunch away from the beach, there are many small restaurants that offer *comida corrida*—a three-course meal consisting of a soup, rice, a choice of hearty main dishes, tortillas, desert, and agua fresca, water blended with fresh fruit and sugar. All is included in one fixed price that is rarely more than $30 pesos.

Dinner

Dinner or *cena* is generally a late affair in Mexico, and traditionally a lighter meal than lunch. However, the Pacific coast resort towns have adapted to the varied dinner hours and styles of travelers here, so you'll find every option available, from 6pm until midnight. Early diners will want to choose a place where they can view the setting sun, and both Puerto Vallarta and Acapulco offer numerous hillside restaurants with expansive views. Later

> In Mexico, a waiter will never bring your check until you request it—after all, the waiter wouldn't want to appear to be unwelcoming, or to be rushing you. Always remember to ask "la cuenta, por favor" (check, please).

diners may choose to enjoy a more formal evening, where sophisticated menus are accompanied by candlelight and the soft music of a romantic trio. There are numerous award-winning restaurants along this stretch of coast, with Puerto Vallarta gaining a reputation for its culinary accomplishments. An annual gourmet dining festival held each November showcases the talents of Vallarta's growing number of European-born chefs who have relocated here, lured by the abundance and variety of fresh ingredients, and the high standard of living.

Dinner may also be a very casual affair. In Acapulco, dinner may consist of tasty seafood tacos along the Costera, or a delicious seafood meal from one of the small family restaurants located near the main square. A culinary tradition in Acapulco—served every Thursday—is the hearty *pozole blanco,* a hominy stew served in a white broth with pork or chicken, and garnished with shredded cabbage, chopped onion, oregano, sliced radishes, and lime. In Puerto Vallarta, pozole is more commonly served in a red broth, which is prepared with *chile guajillo,* a mild, dried pepper.

Fine food, fine company, and a fine tequila... ¡Buen provecho!

So, as you sit down to enjoy your meal, be sure to do as the locals and wish everyone, *"¡Buen provecho!"*

To Help You Order...

Here are a few terms that may enhance your dining experience. Be bold and try to scrape by in Spanish—your efforts will be appreciated.

¿Tiene una mesa para una/dos/tres/cuatro persona/personas?	Do you have a table for one/two/three/four people?

¿Tiene un menú?	Do you have a menu?
¿Cuánto cuesta?	How much is it?
La cuenta, por favor.	The bill, please.

...and Read the Menu

aguacate	avocado
ajo	garlic
bistek	steak
café	coffee
calamares	squid
camarones	shrimp
cebolla	onion
cerdo/puerco	pork
cerveza	beer
chile	peppers
chorizo	spicy pork sausage
ensalada	salad
frijoles	beans
huevos	eggs
leche	milk
mantequilla	butter
mariscos	seafood
pan	bread
pan dulce	sweet rolls/pastries
papas	potatoes
pescado	fish
pollo	chicken
queso	cheese
res	beef
sopa	soup

Mexican specialties

al albañil	with a very spicy sauce

al ajillo	in spicy oil made with red dried pepper (*chile de árbol*)
ceviche	fish or seafood cooked in lime juice and or vinegar, varies in style depending on the region in which it is prepared
en escabeche	pickled
enchiladas	tortillas served in a mole, tomato, or green sauce, filled with chicken or cheese, topped with cream, cheese and onions.
flan	sweet custard made with eggs, milk, and vanilla
guacamole	mashed avocados with onions, peppers, and chile
mole	a spicy sauce made of eleven different ingredients and spices including chiles, chocolate, and almonds
nopales	cactus leaves usually served as a salad, but can be served cooked in a red or green sauce, or grilled.
puntas	beef tips, usually served in a mild sauce
quesadilla	corn or flour tortilla folded in half and filled with cheese; potatoes, mushrooms, shredded beef can be additional fillings.
salsa mexicana	hot sauce made with chopped tomatoes, onions, green peppers, and cilantro
salsa roja	hot sauce made with peppers and tomatoes
salsa verde	hot sauce made with green peppers and green tomatoes, cilantro, and onion
taco	a corn or flour tortilla, stuffed with a variety of fillings
tamal	corn batter stuffed with either sweet or savory fillings that are wrapped in corn husks and steamed

HANDY TRAVEL TIPS

An A–Z Summary of Practical Information

A

ACCOMMODATION (*Alojamiento*)
Hotel prices are generally based on categories that range from lavish (Grand Tourism) to minimal (one star), but ratings often don't tell the whole story. A small, charming independent hotel or bed-and-breakfast may charge lower rates simply because it doesn't have TV or a pool, or is located a few blocks from the beach, while run-of-the-mill hotels that feature such amenities may cost twice as much. Depending on various packages and seasonal discounts, the same lodging may go for very different prices. An experienced travel agent can be a great help in giving advice tailored to your needs.

Rates are higher (and harder to negotiate) from mid-December until Easter, with holiday weeks generally booked well in advance. The most economical accommodations are those in small hotels near the central part of the city, away from the ocean, or around the zócalo, and in the older sections of town.

All beach resorts now feature time-share **apartments and suites,** and many important hotel chains are now partners in time-share developments. **Furnished apartments** (*amueblados o suites*) are an option for longer stays. Check with the local real estate association for recommendations of rental agencies. Local newspapers and community bulletin boards are great places to find longer-term rentals.

I'd like a single/double room	**Quisiera una habitación sencilla/doble**
with bath/shower.	**con baño/regadera**.
What's the rate per night?	**¿Cuál es la tarifa por noche?**
Where is there a cheap hotel?	**¿Dónde hay un hotel barato?**

AIRPORT
Air service to Pacific Coast Mexico is increasing, with Puerto Vallarta and Acapulco airports offering the most options for sched-

uled air and charter flights. If your flight is direct into your final destination you will clear both immigration and customs once you arrive. Most flights still connect through Mexico City, and if your first stop is there, or another city in Mexico, your luggage should be checked through to your final destination. You will, however, need to clear immigration at your first point of entry in Mexico.

Wherever you clear customs, an official will review your declaration and ask you to press a button on something that looks like a traffic light. If you get a green light you walk right through, if you get a red light they will ask you to open your luggage and a brief inspection will take place.

The international airports in Puerto Vallarta, Acapulco, Huatulco, Ixtapa, Manzanillo, and Mazatlán are all small and easy to navigate. Porters are readily available, as are taxis, just as you depart the customs clearance area. Customary tips are about the equivalent of US$1 per bag.

In all airports you will find **casas de cambio** (currency exchange booths, which offer almost the same rates as a bank), where you can exchange travelers checks, dollars, and pesos. There are also newsstands, places to eat and drink, and hotel and travel information services. Public telephones are clearly marked *LADATEL*, and require a debit card for local or long distance calls. The cards can be purchased at stores in the airports.

Every airport has a taxi booth, where authorized taxis can be hired to take you to your destination in town. Only use an "authorized" cab — airport taxis are licensed by the federal government for exclusive use at the airports, and aren't allowed to pick up passengers in town. They usually are yellow and white (mostly white) vehicles marked *transportación terrestre* ("ground transportation"). Generally, both private cabs and a less expensive, shared van service are available. Private cab rates will run US$10 to US$35, compared to about one-third of that price for the in-bound airport service. There is a US$12 airport departure tax that most airlines include in the price of your ticket. It's wise to double-check, to make sure you are not caught by surprise at the airport upon leaving.

Aeropuerto Internacional Gustavo Díaz Ordaz, in Puerto Vallarta (PVR), is located about 5 miles north of the town's center, and only a few blocks from Marina Vallarta. **Aeropuerto Internacional Playa de Oro,** in Manzanillo (ZLO), is located 37.5 km (25 miles) northwest of town. **Aeropuerto Internacional Zihuatanejo,** in Zihuatanejo (ZIH), is located 10 km (7 miles) south of town. **Aeropuerto Internacional Juan N. Alvarez,** in Acapulco (ACA), is located 21 km (14 miles) southeast of town, and **Aeropuerto Internacional Huatulco,** in Huatulco (HUX), is located 18 km (12 miles) northwest of town.

Porter!	**¡Maletero!**
Where's the bus for…?	**¿Dónde se toma el camión para…?**
Where can I get a taxi?	**¿Dónde puedo tomar un taxi?**
I have a connecting flight to…	**Tengo un vuelo de conexión a….**

B

BUDGETING FOR YOUR TRIP

Although beach resorts are more expensive then Mexico's smaller towns and colonial cities, they still offer excellent vacation values. All-inclusive hotels are becoming more common, where the price of your stay includes all meals, beverages, activities, and entertainment. While some resort hotels charge more than 1,500 pesos per night, clean and comfortable accommodations can be found ranging from 250 to 450 pesos per room night. Such rooms are usually for two persons, and it is common for children to be able to stay for free in their parents' room.

Dining is an excellent value when compared to most US or European destinations, with *comidas corridas* (fixed price lunches) costing between 25 and 35 pesos for a full meal.

Transportation inside each town and city is also very reasonable. Most intra-city bus rides rarely cost more than seven pesos, and taxis average about 20 to 30 pesos per short trip within a city. Buses are the most economical option for travel inside Mexico, with long, 1,200 km (720 miles) trips costing around 900 pesos. In comparison, internal flights can be very expensive with air travel between resorts costing up to 8,000 pesos.

C

CAMPING

In Mexico, all beaches are open to the public. However before you decide to camp on the beach, check the surrounding areas and ask advice from the locals. While most beaches are fairly safe, it is a good idea to take precautions, since campers are easy targets for muggings. Favored areas are in San Francisco (also known as San Pancho), located one hour north of Puerto Vallarta, and in the pristine bays of Huatulco. For information about camping and a complete list of campgrounds and trailer parks call **INFOTUR** at Tel. (800) 482-9832 inside the US, Tel. 01-800-903-9200 or (5) 250-0123 inside Mexico, or write to:

> INFOTUR
> Presidente Mazaryk 172
> Col. Polanco, México, D.F., CP 11587.

May we camp here?	**¿Podemos acampar aquí?**
We have a tent/trailer.	**Tenemos una tienda de campaña/ un trailer.**

CAR RENTAL/HIRE *(Arrendamiento de Automóviles)*

Car rental prices are relatively high in Mexico. All well-known international companies and many reliable national ones rent cars and jeeps to adults with a valid driver's license and a credit card (you must have a credit card in order to rent). The driver must be at least 18 years of age. It is advisable to take the insurance option, and many companies will automatically include this in their prices. Rates vary, but you can expect to pay US$50 to US$80 per day with unlimited mileage. Pay close attention to the pre-rental damage report, and be sure all scratches and dents are recorded.

If you are staying in one place — say Acapulco or Puerto Vallarta — there is no real need to rent a car, as parking is quite difficult and taxis are inexpensive. You can frequently hire a taxi with driver for a day at almost the same price as a rental car would cost. A car is advisable if you're traveling along the Costa Alegre, or to Puerto Escondido from Huatulco. Many companies will allow you to drop the car at a destination other than your point of departure, for a small, additional charge. See also "Driving" and "Crime and Safety."

I'd like to rent a car for today/tomorrow.	**Quisiera rentar un coche para hoy/mañana.**
for one day/one week.	**Por un día/una semana**
With insurance	**Con seguro**

CLIMATE

The weather along the Mexican Pacific Coast is typically tropical, ranging from perfect to quite hot and humid. Puerto Vallarta has beautiful weather from November through April with cool mornings and evenings. Temperatures may drop to 15°C, while days are sunny, warm, and clear, with average temperatures of 22°C. The farther south you travel, the hotter the average temperatures are. While Puerto Vallarta can get into the high 30s between August and October, temperature rarely reaches 40°C, which is normal during the summer months in Zihuatanejo, Acapulco, and destinations located farther down the coast. Rainy season occurs between May and October, with brief but strong afternoon thunderstorms cooling off the evenings. Southern beaches see the most action during hurricane season, with September and October having some very strong storms at least once a year.

Temperature

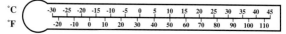

CLOTHING

Light, informal summer clothing is fine for all beach resorts year-round, but you should bring a light sweater and windbreaker for the occasional cool morning and evening. A light raincoat or umbrella will come in handy from May to October. Ties and jackets for men are virtually unknown at beach resorts. Don't wear extra-short miniskirts or shorts (the latter goes for men as well) anywhere in Mexico apart from the big tourist resorts. It is never appropriate to enter a church wearing bathing suits or short-shorts. As a general rule, in the more remote and smaller villages both men and women should dress conservatively. Sandals as well as a comfortable pair of walking shoes are a must. Note: Mexico has laws prohibiting nude or topless sunbathing on its beaches, although custom permits it in a few select areas, such as Zipolite beach, located north of Huatulco.

COMPLAINTS *(Reclamación)*

If you have a complaint against a hotel, restaurant, taxi driver, time-share company, or tourist guide, and you can't resolve it on the spot, go to the Procuraduría Federal del Consumidor (Profeco). There is a local Profeco office in all major destinations within Mexico. In Puerto Vallarta call Tel. (3) 225-0018, or (3) 225-0000; in Acapulco call Tel. (7) 483-5233, or (7) 483-9358. A word of caution — registering a complaint is usually a long and frustrating process. Quite often there is no English-speaking personnel, and the declaration itself may take hours. Because these procedures require court hearings, authorities will not make any ruling until a hearing takes place. Many cases are dropped, because by the time the hearings are set up, the person making the complaint has returned home.

I have a complaint　　　　　　**Tengo una queja**

CRIME AND SAFETY

Mexico's Pacific coast resorts are generally considered very safe, with the exception of the highways outside of Acapulco (see page 110). The most frequent crime is petty theft, and pickpockets tend to operate wherever there are crowds. Be alert. There is a brisk trade in US passports. Don't leave yours in the hotel room — use the hotel safe for valuables, and use the chain lock when inside your hotel room. Always lock your car; don't leave valuables in sight. Don't leave luggage or packages unattended. Women should avoid purses with large openings that do not zip or have a flap that can be secured. Throughout the Mexican Pacific, it is advised that you not carry valuables to the beach, especially more secluded beaches.

In Puerto Escondido, instances of assault and rape were occurring with enough frequency to inspire local authorities to install stadium-style lighting along the main beaches. Travelers are urged to be cautious, and avoid walking alone or in secluded areas at night.

To report a crime to the local Mexican authorities, dial the 060 emergency number (similar to 911 in the US). The Procuraduría del Turista was created to help tourists who are victims of crimes. To contact them call Tel. (5) 625-8153 or (5) 625-8154 in Mexico City; or (7) 484-4583 and (7) 484-4416 in Acapulco. In Puerto Vallarta, the Seguridad Pública (Tel. (3) 221-2586, (3) 221-2587, and (3) 221-2588) handles reports of violent crimes. There is also an Agencia Especial para Turistas (Tel. (3) 223-0470), where English-speaking personnel will take your report and start the proceedings.

If you are victim of a crime, or feel you have been unfairly treated by the police, make sure you report it to your consular office (see page 112 for telephone information).

Warning: In some cases, the people to be wary of are the police themselves. In Puerto Vallarta it has become a common practice for police officers to randomly frisk anyone they suspect of carrying drugs. Although this is technically in violation of the Mexican constitution, most of those who object seem to get an automatic ride to jail for resisting. A small fine of about 150 pesos will be required for your release.

Make sure you stay away from illegal drugs — they are not tolerated in Mexico. If you are caught in possession of illegal substances, it will be practically impossible to avoid jail, and most of what you have heard about Mexican jails is true — they are that bad. If the Federal Police pick you up, even on suspicion of drug possession or dealing, you can be held for an extended period of time without trial.

I want to report a theft	**Quiero denunciar(reportar) un robo.**

CUSTOMS AND ENTRY FORMALITIES

Formalities at a border or airport are quick and simple. Instead of a visa, visitors must have a **tourist card,** obtainable upon proof of citizenship from airlines serving Mexico and at border points. The card is valid for three months and is renewable for another three. The tourist card will be stamped upon entry and it must be kept with you for presentation on departure. If you lose it, report this to the local immigration office at once to avoid delays on departure. Tourists may visit Mexico for 72 hours without a tourist card and without paying the US$15 visitor's tax. See also "Airports."

You may bring into Mexico 12 rolls of film or videocassettes, 500 cigarettes or 100 cigars or 250 grams of pipe tobacco, and three liters of spirits or wine.

The following chart shows the main duty-free items you may bring into your own country when returning home.

	Cigarettes		Cigars		Tobacco	Spirits		Wine
Australia	250	or	200	or	250g	1.1l	or	1.1l
Canada	200	or	50	and	1 kg	1.1l	or	1.1l
Ireland	200	or	50	or	250g	1l	or	2l
N. Zealand	200	or	50	or	250g	1.1l	and	4.5l

S. Africa	400	and	50	and	250g	ll	and	2l
UK	200	or	50	or	250g	ll	and	2l
US	200	and	50	and	*	ll	and	ll

*A reasonable quantity

Currency restrictions. Non-residents may import or export any amount of freely convertible foreign currency into Mexico provided it is declared upon arrival. There is also no limit to the amount of Mexican currency you may carry into or out of Mexico.

I have nothing to declare.   **No tengo nada que declarar.**

D

DRIVING
Any valid driver's license is accepted in Mexico. If you are driving into Mexico in your own car, you must present proof of ownership at the border, where it will be registered with your tourist card. A small duty, or bond, is also charged upon entry into Mexico, to ensure you will not be selling your car inside the country. Only the owner of the car can drive it, otherwise you need to have a notarized letter stating the names of those who will be driving. Take out full accident and liability Mexican insurance at the border, since insurance from other countries usually does not apply.

Road conditions. Most Mexican surfaced roads have only two lanes; mountain roads are very winding, often without shoulders. While the main highways and expressways are generally in good condition, be careful rounding curves and topping rises. Avoid driving at night, as few public roads have lights. Rocks or branches on the road mean there's a broken down vehicle ahead, or a huge pothole on the middle of the road.

Rules and regulations. Get a good road map from your automobile club (they are not sold in petrol stations). Look out for signs in villages and near schools announcing *topes* or *vibradores,* speed bumps placed across the road to slow traffic. Sometimes they are hard to spot, so keep your eyes open. "E" (*estacionamiento*) in a circle with a line through it means "No Parking." When approaching a narrow bridge, the first car to flash its lights has right of way.

Fuel costs. The average cost per liter is about 43 cents (US$1.65) per gallon. Pemex is the federal supplier, and while fuel is still distributed through the government only, petrol stations are now concessions and the new ones usually include well-stocked convenience stores and restrooms that are reasonably clean. There are two kinds of fuel: unleaded *magna* with an 83 octane level, and *premium* with 97 octane. Octane ratings are not the same as in the US and sometimes they slow the combustion, so an additive is advisable. Fill up whenever your tank is half-empty; it may be a long drive to the next station. Credit cards are not accepted at petrol stations. Station attendants should be tipped.

Parking. In Puerto Vallarta, Acapulco, and the other principal Pacific coast resorts, parking is generally on-street, and can be difficult to find in the more congested downtown areas. Most hotels offer secured parking for their guests.

If you need help. If you have car trouble, raise your hood and wait for the "Green Angels" (*Angeles Verdes*). These green government repair trucks patrol the main routes from 8am to 7pm, making minor repairs and supplying emergency fuel. They charge only the cost of the materials, but tips are also appropriate. It is a good idea to bring along any spare parts such as a fan belt and oil filter, which may be difficult to obtain.

Special travel advisory. Car robberies and bus hijackings on Highway 200 south of Acapulco are frequent, making this an unsafe route, even though occasional military checkpoints have been installed. If you're traveling south from Acapulco, it's much safer to fly.

Road Signs: Most Mexican road signs are standard international pictographs. But you may encounter these written signs:

Aduana	Customs
Alto	Stop
Autopista (de cuota)	(Toll) highway
Camino deteriorado (en malas condiciones)	Bad road
Ceda el paso	Yield
Crucero peligroso	Dangerous crossing
Cuidado	Caution
Curva peligrosa	Dangerous curve
Despacio	Slow
Desviación	Detour
Escuela	School
Peligro	Danger
Prohibido estacionarse	No parking
Prohibido (No) rebasar	No passing
Puesto de socorro	First-aid station
Puente angosto	Narrow bridge
Salida de camiones	Truck exit

Other Useful Phrases:

(International) driver's license	**Licencia para manejar (internacional)**
Car registration papers	**Registro del automovil**
Are we on the right road for…?	**¿Es esta la carretera hacia…?**

Puerto Vallarta & Acapulco

Fill the tank, top grade, please. **Llénelo, con premium, por favor**

Check the oil/tires/battery **Revise el aceite/las llantas /la batería**

I've had a breakdown. **Mi carro se ha descompuesto**

There's been an accident **Ha habido un accidente**

Fluid measures

Distance

ELECTRICITY

Mexico uses the US and Canadian system of 120 volts, 60 cycles; however, two flat pins are commonly used in wall plugs, so a 3- to 2-prong adapter can be handy. Appliances using the European system will require a transformer as well as an adapter plug. Voltage variations are very common, so a surge protector and regulator is recommended if you are using any personal computer equipment.

EMBASSIES AND CONSULATES

Embassies:

Australia Rubén Dario 55, Col. Polanco, Mexico City, CP 11580; Tel. (5) 531-5225

Canada Schiller 529, Colonia Polanco, Mexico City, CP 11570; Tel. (5) 724-7900

New Zealand José Luis LaGrange103, 10th floor, Col. Polanco, Mexico City, CP 11570; Tel. (5) 281-5486

South Africa AndresBello 10, 9th floor, Col. Polanco, Mexico City, CP 11510; Tel (5) 282-9260

UK Rio Usumacinta 30, Col. Cuauhtemoc, Mexico City, CP 06500; Tel. (5) 207-2089

US Paseo de la Reforma 305, Col. Cuauhtemoc, Mexico City, CP 06500; Tel. (5) 209-9100

Consulates:

Canada Centro Comercial Marbella, Local 23, Prolongación Farallón S/N, Acapulco, Guerrero; Tel. (7) 484-1305

Zaragoza 160, Interior 10, Col. Centro, Puerto Vallarta, Jalisco CP 48300; Tel. (3) 222-5398

UK Hotel Las Brisas, Carretera Escenica 5255, Acapulco, Guerrero, CP 39868; Tel. (7) 484-6605

CEPROTUR, Plaza Santo Domingo Int 13, Alcalá and Allende, Oaxaca, CP 68000; Tel. (9) 516-7280

US Hotel Acapulco Continental, Office 14, Acapulco, Guerrero, CP 39580; Tel. (7) 481-1699

Plaza Ambiente, Ixtapa, Zihutanejo, Guerrero, CP 40880; Tel. (7) 553-1108

Vallarta Building, Zaragoza 160, 2nd floor, Puerto Vallarta, Jalisco, CP 48300; Tel. (3) 222-0069

EMERGENCIES

In case of an emergency, dial **060** to contact the local police. If you are the victim of a crime first report it to the police and then contact your embassy or the closest consular office immediately. Most hotel rooms will have local telephone directories with emergency numbers for the local fire department and ambulance service listed on the first pages.

Help!	**Auxilio! Ayúdenme!**
Call the police!	**Llamen a la policia!**
Get an ambulance!	**Llamen a una ambulancia!**
Get a doctor!	**Llamen a un doctor!**

G

GAY AND LESBIAN TRAVELERS

Due to its conservative, predominantly Catholic culture, Mexico is a place where same-sex couples are not openly accepted. Public displays of affection, especially between men, are rare and still considered shocking. Despite that, the resort areas of Acapulco, Puerto Vallarta, and Ixtapa are essentially welcoming to gay and lesbian travelers. Puerto Vallarta is known as the most gay-friendly destination in Mexico, with a selection of accommodations and entertainment oriented especially toward same-sex couples. In Los Muertos beach, the stretch of beach known as "blue chairs" is a very popular gay meeting place. The free, monthly *PV Southside Guide* (www .pvsouthside.com; Tel. (52) 3/221-0297) is gay-oriented, with listings of special events, as well as gay-friendly restaurants, nightlife, and activities. A special travel service, Doin' it Right in Puerto Vallarta (Tel. 800/936-3646, 619/297-3642) rents gay-friendly condos and villas for individuals and groups. The newsletter is also available by e-mail: GayPVR@aol.com.

GETTING THERE

Most international flights will first arrive in Mexico City or Guadalajara, before continuing on to the Pacific coast, although Puerto Vallarta and Acapulco have an increasing number of direct flights. International airlines have service into Mexico from almost every major airport in the US, with most direct flights arriving from New York, Chicago, Los Angeles, Dallas, Houston, and Miami. Overseas airports with direct flights to Mexico City include Frankfurt, London, Paris, Amsterdam, and Madrid. Numerous US- and Canadian-based tour operators offer less expensive charter flights to Mexico Pacific resorts, especially during the winter vacation season.

HEALTH AND MEDICAL CARE

No vaccinations are required for entry to Mexico, but your doctor may recommend updating your tetanus and polio immunizations and suggest gamma globulin as a hepatitis deterrent.

The most notorious Mexican health hazard, known to tourists as *turista* or "Moctezuma's Revenge" is a relatively harmless combination of diarrhea and upset stomach, caused usually by the difference in chemicals and bacteria in drinking water. The best way to avoid this nuisance is to refrain from drinking tap water and consume only purified bottled water. Take ice only in places where you are quite sure that it is made from purified water, or ask for drinks *sin hielo* (without ice). Avoid raw fruits or vegetables unless they can be peeled, and food sold at street stands. If you do succumb, take plenty of liquids with a little salt and sugar. Herbal teas like *manzanilla* (chamomile), or sports drinks like Gatorade will replenish some of the minerals you loose.

In almost every tourist destination there are pharmacies open 24 hours a day that deliver without extra charge. There are pharmacies that remain "on duty" after hours, on weekends, and holidays. Most first class hotels have a doctor on call who speaks English. Consular offices will have a list of doctors who speak English and other languages.

In resorts such as Puerto Vallarta, Huatulco, and Acapulco, several of the larger private hospitals are set up to accept US insurance coverage, as long as payment is guaranteed by credit card as well. Prices for medical services are significantly below equivalent charges in the US.

Get me a doctor, quickly!   **¡Llamen a un médico, rápido!**

LANGUAGE

Mexico is the largest Spanish-speaking country in the world. In addition, Mexican Indians speak 58 indigenous languages or dialects, with Spanish as their *lingua franca*. English is understood in hotels and tourist-oriented establishments throughout the country. But any Spanish phrases you learn will be appreciated by Mexicans and will make asking directions, shopping, and ordering food easier.

The Berlitz phrase book, *Latin–American Spanish for Travelers*, covers most situations you are likely to encounter in your visit to Mexico; also useful is the Berlitz English-Spanish pocket dictionary, containing a special menu-reader supplement. (See also "Eating Out," page 92.)

MEDIA

Most daily newspapers in Mexico City are heavily oriented toward local and national events. Two English dailies, *The News* and the *Mexico City News*, are distributed across the country. Foreign magazines are easy to find in drugstores and tobacco shops at hotels and airports.

Most hotels offer cable or satellite TV with at least one US channel (such as CNN) that broadcasts current news. Stereorey is a predominantly English-language music FM station with broadcast affiliates in most of Mexico.

In Puerto Vallarta, there are two English-language community newspapers: the daily *Vallarta Today*, and the weekly *Tribune*. In addition, the quarterly bilingual *Vallarta Lifestyles* magazine is sold throughout town.

Have you any English- language
newspapers/magazines?

**¿Tiene periódicos/
revistas en inglés?**

MONEY MATTERS

The currency of Mexico is the **peso**, designated by the international sign for currency: $ (in this book we have not used the $ sign for the peso, to avoid confusion with the US$). A peso is divided into 100 centavos, but you will only find 20 and 50 centavos coins, and usually prices are rounded to the closest peso amount: instead of something being 1.50 (one peso and fifty centavos) it will be 2 pesos. There are also coins worth 1, 5, and 10 pesos. Bills are issued in 20, 50, 100, 200, and 500 pesos. The bills have different sizes and colors. Be careful not to accept bills that are torn, ripped, taped or otherwise damaged, as neither businesses nor banks will accept them.

Banking hours are normally Monday through Friday from 9am to 5pm. Several banks offer extended hours until 7pm, and others open on Saturdays from 10am to 2pm. Banks will exchange foreign currency during banking hours. Keep in mind that banks are usually crowded on the 1st, 15th, and last day of the month — payday for most employees.

Most banks now have **ATMs**, where you can withdraw funds from your bank account in pesos (or sometimes in dollars), usually at a favorable exchange rate. Be cautious when using these machines, and try to limit use to daylight hours, in busier areas.

Credit cards are widely accepted, though not in petrol stations. US dollars and traveler's checks are often accepted in resort areas and airports.

Exchange rates. All banks offer the same rate, published daily in Mexico City. Some banks charge a 1% fee to exchange traveler's checks (you will need your passport as an ID). Private exchanges (casas de cambio) will exchange currency and travelers checks at or near bank rates, and are open longer hours and on many holidays. Try to keep small change, such as 5- and 10-peso coins for tipping, paying taxis, and making small purchases. Hotels exchange money at disadvantageous rates.

I want to change some dollars/pounds	**Quiero cambiar dólares/ libras esterlinas**

Puerto Vallarta & Acapulco

Do you accept traveler's checks?   **¿Acepta cheques de viajero?**

Can I pay with this credit card?   **¿Puedo pagar con esta tarjeta de crédito?**

OPENING HOURS
In most towns shops and offices usually close between 2pm and 4pm and then remain open until 7pm or 8pm in the evening. As a rule the larger the city the longer the business hours. Sunday is still the revered day off in Mexico; most offices and shops are closed, and the beaches will be the most crowded.

POLICE
There are several branches of the police in Mexico: the local or municipal police; their traffic division, in charge of all traffic-related incidents; and the state, federal, and judicial police. Each has a different jurisdiction, but in case of an incident where the intervention of the police is required, any passing patrol can offer assistance.

Everywhere in Mexico, dial 060 or 080 for emergency police assistance; however, most operators are not bilingual. Remember to always call the nearest embassy or consular office if you are involved in any incident that requires that you contact the police. See also "Crime and Safety."

POST OFFICES (*Correos*)
The Mexican Postal Service is still notoriously slow in delivery. Airmail (*correo aereo*) takes close to three weeks to get to the US, and longer to get to Canada and Europe (always put international mail in the *Aereo* slot). It costs only 4.20 pesos to mail either a postcard or a letter to the US (mail to Canada and Europe costs slightly more). Opening hours are usually from 9am to 6pm, closing at 1pm on Saturdays.

stamp / letter / postcard	**timbre-estampilla/carta/ tarjeta postal**
special delivery (express)	**urgente**
mailbox	**buzón**
airmail	**correo aéreo**
surface mail	**correo terrestre**
registered	**registrado**

PUBLIC HOLIDAYS *(Día Festivo)*

January 1	*Año Nuevo* (New Year's Day}
February 5	*Aniversario de la Constitución* (Constitution Day)
March 21	*Natalicio de Benito Juárez* (Birthday of Benito Juárez)
Movable date	*Semana Santa y Pascua* (Easter)
May 1	*Día del Trabajo* (Labor day)
May 5	*Batalla de Puebla* (Battle of Puebla)
September 1	Informe Presidencial (President's Address)
September 16	*Día de la Independencia* (Independence Day)
October 12	*Día de la Raza* (Columbus Day)
November 2	*Día de Muertos* (All Soul's Day)
November 20	*Aniversario de la Revolución* (Anniversary of the Mexican Revolution)

December 12   *Nuestra Señora de Guadalupe*
                         (Our Lady of Guadalupe)

December 25   *Navidad* (Christmas)

PUBLIC TRANSPORTATION

Public buses are efficient and inexpensive. Fares are generally 3 to 7 pesos. Most buses will have the route marked on the front window. When you want to get off, press a buzzer or pull a cord in advance of the stop, or call out "¡bajan, por favor!" (down, please!) Buses are commonly crowded during rush hours, and rarely are air-conditioned.

 R

RELIGION

Mexico is a predominantly Roman Catholic country; however, there are Protestant churches in most cities. Churches in larger cities and resort areas often have Sunday services in English. Most resort towns offer Sunday mass in English at different hotels.

What time is mass/the service? **¿A qué hora es la misa/
                                 el servicio?**

Is it in English?   **¿Es en inglés?**

 T

TAXIS

Taxis are normally not expensive, but generally do not have meters; make a practice of asking drivers how much the ride will cost before starting out, to avoid any unpleasant surprises.

Check with your hotel to find out about typical cab fares. Most taxi drivers will also offer their services on an hourly basis to drive you around and show the interesting sites (even waiting for you while you go shopping or sight-seeing). The average rate is around 100 pesos per hour. As a rule the federally chartered taxis *from* the airport are twice or three times as expensive as taxis within a town, so expect to pay much more for the ride from the airport to your hotel than the ride back.

What's the fare to…?   **¿Cual es la tarifa a…?**

TELEPHONE

Mexico's country code is 52. Public phones operated by Telmex, are gray booths and have *LADATEL* written on them. They are the most economical choice for all types of calling. They operate with debit cards, which can be purchased in drugstores and convenience stores in denominations of 30, 50, and 100 pesos. You need a card with debit even if you are calling a toll-free number.

Throughout Mexico dial the following: 040 (information, directory assistance), 060 (police/emergency), 090 (international operator), and 020 (national operator).

Long distance dialing. As a rule long distance calls are very expensive. Hotels charge extra for long distance calls, so you are better off calling collect from your hotel. Dial 090 from any phone to make a collect call. All person-to-person and collect calls must be made through an operator.

Beware of predatory phones advertising credit-card calls to the US and Canada — these services charge exorbitant rates.

To make a long distance call within Mexico dial 01 + area code + number (a total of 10 numbers).

To make a long distance call to the US or Canada dial 001 + area code + number.

To make a long distance call to the rest of the world dial 00 + country code + area code + number.

Can you dial this number?   **¿Puede comunicarme a este número?**

Collect call (reverse-charge)   **por cobrar**

Person-to-person call (personal) **de persona a persona**

TIME DIFFERENCES

Most of Mexico, and all places discussed in this book, are on Central
Standard Time (GMT minus six hours). Since 1996 it is customary
to adjust for daylight savings time during the summer.

What time is it?   **¿Qué hora es?**

TIPPING

Wages are low in Mexico and most service-oriented employees count on
tips to make up the majority of their income. This is especially true for
bellhops and waiters. Bellhops receive the equivalent of 50 cents to US$1
per bag; waiters generally receive 10 to 20%, depending on the level of
service; some restaurants include the tip in the bill, especially when serving large parties, so check to make sure. Maids receive between US$4
and US$10 per week depending on the service and the rating of the ho-
tel. Other services are tipped according to the level of service — 10 to
20% of the cost of the service provided. In Mexico, it is not customary
to tip taxi drivers unless they are hired by the hour, or provide touring
or other special services. It is customary to tip tour guides.

Keep the change.   **Es para usted.**

TOILETS

In Mexico toilets may be referred to as *baños, sanitarios, tocadores,
escusados,* or WC. The doors may be labeled *caballeros* or H (*hom-
bres*) for men, and M (*mujeres*) or *damas* for women. Sometimes
there are flowers and trees, or suns and moons, rather than words to
differentiate the gender. Progress has been made recently in keeping
public toilets clean, but carrying tissues with you is still advisable. If
there is an attendant who hands you towels, a small tip is expected.

Where are the toilets?   **¿Dónde están los baños?**

TOURIST INFORMATION OFFICES (*Oficinas de Turismo*)

The Mexican government maintains many tourist offices abroad; in addition, any Mexican consulate will provide information about travel to

Mexico and, in many cases, house full-fledged tourism offices. Information is also available on the Internet at: www.mexico-travel.com.

Following is a list of the **Mexican Government Tourism Offices**:

Canada

1 Place Ville-Marie, Suite 1931, Montréal, QUEB, H3B 2C3; Tel. (514) 871-1052

2 Bloor St. W., Suite 1502, Toronto, ON, M4W 3E2; Tel. (416) 925-2753

999 W. Hastings, Suite 1110, Vancouver, BC, V6C 2W2; Tel. (604) 669-2845

UK

60/61 Trafalgar Square, London WC2 N5D5; Tel. (171) 734-1050

US

300 N. Michigan Ave, 3rd floor, Chicago, IL 60601; Tel. (312) 606-9252

1200 N.W. 78th Ave., Suite 203, Miami, FL 33126; Tel. (305) 443-9160

21 E. 63rd St., 3rd. floor, New York, NY 10021; Tel. (800) 446-3942, (212) 421-6655

Mexican Embassy Tourism Delegate, 1911 Pennsylvania Ave., Washington, DC 20005; Tel. (202) 728-1750

You can get a list of the local Tourism Offices in the places you are planing to visit by calling SECTUR's toll-free number from the US: 800-482-9832, or by dialing (5) 250-0123 in Mexico City.

INFOTUR is a service offered by SECTUR, providing bilingual tourist information. The toll-free number inside Mexico is 01-800-903-9200; from the US, dial 1-800-482-9832; in Mexico City, call (5) 250-0123.

| Where is the nearest tourist office? | **¿Dónde está la oficina de turismo más cercana?** |

WEB SITES

It is getting easier to find information about traveling to Mexico through the Internet, however there is still a long way to go before it is as efficient and up to date as in more developed countries. Official sites are run by government offices and tourism boards, but they are generally not updated frequently, and the links to other sites often don't work. Private sites seem to be updated with much greater frequency, but are not comprehensive, since only paying advertisers are included. Following is a list of the official sites and some of the more comprehensive private sites.

www.mexico-travel.com The official site of Mexico's Ministry of Tourism includes an enormous amount of official information and travel tips about all of Mexico.

www.puertovallarta.net The site of the Puerto Vallarta Tourism Board has basic information about events, attractions, and accommodations in Puerto Vallarta and a comprehensive list of links to related Vallarta information.

www.acapulco-cvb.org The site of Acapulco's Convention and Visitor Bureau has information about activities, accommodations, tours, restaurants, nightlife, and more, with some links to related private sites.

www.BaysOfHuatulco.com.mx The site of Huatulcos' Fondo Mixto currently available only in Spanish, has a wealth of information, especially about ecological and cultural attractions.

www.amtave.com. The site of the official organization representing companies and projects involved in eco-tourism in Mexico has links to several tour providers in the Pacific coast.

www.go2mexico.com. An extensive private site with access to current information about many destinations in Mexico; it is easy to navigate and frequently updated.

www.mexconnect.com. An electronic magazine about Mexico with helpful articles on different regions of Mexico.

In addition to these sites there are the popular sites that offer cheap airline tickets and other online bargains: **www.expedia.com, www. all-hotels.com, www.travelocity.com,** and **www.bestfares.com.**

WEIGHTS AND MEASURES

Length

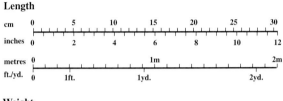

Weight

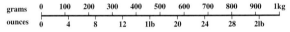

WHEN TO GO

The most popular times to travel to this area are from mid-December through mid-April, when the climate is the most agreeable — warm, sunny, and dry. Other good times to travel are when values are excellent, including mid-April through June, and October through mid-December. You'll enjoy pleasant weather, with fewer crowds at these times. July through mid-August is peak family vacation time within Mexico, so places get crowded. September tends to be the most humid month, with occassional heavy storms.

YOUTH HOSTELS

Mexico has a network of youth hostels (*albergues de la juventud*) through the youth tourism program (*programa de turismo juvenil*) with over 300 associated hotels and hostels. For information contact: Instituto Mexicano de la Juventud–Turismo Juvenil, Serapio Rendón #76, Col. San Rafael, México, D.F., CP 06470

Recommended Hotels

The Mexican Pacific Coast has hotels to fit every budget, size, location, and style preference. Starting from the north and working our way south along the coast, here are some noteworthy choices, based on value for price, or significant for architecture, amenities, or other unique features. Many included here are offered as part of vacation packages; however, all welcome independent travelers. The well-known chain hotels are present along this coast, but this listing focuses on the more unusual choices. Reservations are recommended, and are absolutely necessary around Easter and Christmas holidays. Prices indicated are rack rates for a standard room, based on double occupancy, in US$, for high season—December 15 through April 15—and do not include taxes, which vary between 15% and 17%. Prices drop approximately 15% to 30% during off-season, and special packages offer discounts of up to 40% off rack rates. You might be able to negotiate better prices at the less expensive hotels if you pay in advance or are planning a prolonged stay. Remember to always ask to speak to the owner or manager and get the deal in writing, along with a receipt when you are paying in advance. Most of the listed hotels allow two children under 12 in the same room at no extra charge. Unless noted, all hotels have a pool and air-conditioned rooms. Major credit cards mean Visa, MasterCard, and American Express.

$$$$$	over US$200
$$$$	US$120 US–US$200
$$$	US$80–US$120
$$	US$40–US$80
$	less than US$40

North of Puerto Vallarta

Four Seasons Resort at Punta Mita $$$$$ *Ramal Carretera Federal 200, Km. 19, La Cruz de Huanacaxtle–Punta Mita; Tel. (3) 291 6000; fax (3) 291 6060.* The most luxurious accommodations in the area, with rooms decorated in a muted Huichol theme, set against a backdrop of azure waters and tranquil gardens. On site is a spectacular Jack Nicklaus–designed 18-hole golf course, fine restaurants, and a luxury spa with full services. Wheelchair access. 100 rooms. Major credit cards.

Paradise Village Beach Resort Marina & Spa, Nuevo Vallarta $$$$ *Paseo de los Cocoteros 001; Tel. (3) 226-6770; fax (3) 226 6713.* An all-suite resort with a European spa, marina, tennis, complete shopping area with supermarket, two large pools—one with waterslides and Jacuzzi. All suites have fully equipped kitchens, large private balconies, and marble baths. An 18-hole golf course is scheduled for completion in 2001. Wheelchair access. 490 rooms. Major credit cards.

Puerto Vallarta

Camino Real Puerto Vallarta $$$$ *Carretera a Barra de Navidad Km 3.5; Tel. (3) 221 5000; fax (3) 221 6000.* A grand hotel with the best beach in Puerto Vallarta, located on a private cove. Loyal guests return year after year. All rooms have vibrant color accents in bright yellow and blue in the style of Mexican master architect Legorreta. Several restaurants. Wheelchair access. 337 rooms. Major credit cards.

Hacienda Cora $$$$$ *Pelicanos 311; Tel. (3) 221 0800; fax (3) 221 0801.* A beautiful, small, exclusive inn with highly personalized service. It sits on the edge of the Marina Vallarta Golf

Course, one block from the beach. Rooms feature an elegant décor in light tones of pink and beige, with unique accents. Wheelchair access. 67 rooms.

Hotel Molino de Agua $$$ *Ignacio L. Vallarta 130, Col. Emiliano Zapata; Tel. (3) 222 1957; fax (3) 222 6056.* Wonderfully located adjacent to the Río Cuale, fronting the northern edge of Los Muertos beach. This hotel manages to maintain a quiet atmosphere, with its brick and stucco bungalows spread amid spacious gardens. Rooms are simply appointed in Mexican colonial style. Two pools. 52 rooms. Major credit cards.

Playa Los Arcos $$$ *Olas Altas 380, Col. Emiliano Zapata; Tel. (3) 222-1583; fax (3) 222-2418.* A terrific location in the middle of the Olas Altas neighborhood action, on Los Muertos beach. Simple rooms provide necessary comforts; most have private balconies or terraces with garden or ocean views. 175 rooms. Major credit cards.

Quinta María Cortez $$$$ *Sagitario 132, Conchas Chinas; Tel. (3) 221-5317; fax (3) 221-5327.* An eclectic B&B by the sea, with a singular display of antiques, original art, and Mexican curios in each room. Open to the ocean breezes (no A/C) on its own lovely cove, there's a common area with a small pool, where breakfast is served. Most suites have small kitchenettes and spacious terraces. Close to town; not appropriate for children. 7 rooms. Major credit cards.

Velas Vallarta Grand Suite Resort $$$$ *Paseo de la Marina Norte 585; Tel. (3) 221-0091; fax (3) 221-0751.* Ideal for families. Each spacious suite comes with a completely equipped kitchen, and all have large balconies. The lush, tropical landscaping and large swimming pool with plenty of activities more than makes up for the narrow beach. Mini-supermarket, full spa, two restaurants, and tennis courts on-site; the golf course is directly across the street. Wheelchair access. 324 rooms. Major credit cards.

Costa Alegre

Hotelito Desconocido $$$$$ *Playón de Mismaloya s/n, La Cruz de Loreto; Tel. (3) 298-5209; fax (3) 298-5109.* Located 1 ¹/₂ hours south of Vallarta, this secluded, eco-conscious retreat —with no electricity—is a magical mixture of a luxurious camp and a castaway island. Rooms have private open-air showers, ample beds under gauzy mosquito nets, and wide terraces. All meals and activities are included. Spa services and all drinks are extra. 24 rooms. Major credit cards.

Punta Serena $$$$$ *Carretera Federal 200 Km. 20, Tenacatita; Tel. (3) 351-5013; fax (3) 351 5013.* An all-inclusive resort for adults only, with a holistic approach to relaxation. All meals are vegetarian, and there is no smoking. Activities include tai-chi, yoga, meditation, and the Aztec purification ceremony of the Temazcal. Rooms are basic, yet comfortable, with large balconies or terraces. Cliff-side hot-tubs, small pool, and private beach. 21 rooms. Major credit cards.

The Tamarindo $$$$$ *Km 7.5 Carretera Barra de Navidad–Puerto Vallarta; Tel. (3) 351-5032; fax (3) 351-5070.* An eco-sensitive resort that redefines elegance in its simplicity, service, and attention to detail. Private bungalows have splash pools, ample terraces and living areas. Bedrooms have beautiful wood detailing and oversize bathrooms, which can be closed off for cooling. This hideaway caters to couples looking for seclusion and relaxation. 18-hole golf course. 28 rooms. Major credit cards.

Manzanillo

Camino Real Las Hadas $$$$ *Av. Vista Hermosa y de los Riscos s/n, Fracc. Península de Santiago; Tel. (3) 334-0000; fax 333-10121.* This luxurious resort—elegantly done in a Moorish style "a la Mexicaine"—brought Manzanillo to the attention of the international jet-set. It remains Manzanillo's most romantic setting. Rooms vary in size and appeal, located on terraced levels overlooking the sea. Several restaurants, tennis courts, and an 18-hole golf course are on-site. 233 rooms. Major credit cards.

Hotel Colonial $ *Av. México 100 y González Bocanegra, Centro. Tel. (3) 332-1080; fax (3) 332-1080.* One block from the main square, this colonial-style favorite is a great value, with consistently good service. Simple clean rooms have tile floors, and private baths with showers. A courtyard restaurant/bar is on the ground floor. 38 rooms. Major credit cards.

Kármina Palace $$$$$ *Boulevard Miguel de la Madrid s/n, Península de Santiago; Tel. (3) 334-1313; fax (3) 334-1108.* Probably the best value in an all-inclusive resort in Mexico, with superb attention to detail. Buildings (slightly overdone to resemble Mayan pyramids), are set amid gardens, eight interconnecting swimming pools, three restaurants, a complete spa and gym. All rooms are large, with two big-screen TVs, oversize bathrooms, and private balconies or terraces. Excellent for families. 324 rooms. Major credit cards.

Acapulco

Hotel Grand Meigas Acapulco $$$$ *Cerro San Martín 325, Fracc. Las Playas; Tel. (7) 483-9940; fax (7) 483-9125.*

This all-inclusive resort with a traditional Mexican family ambiance, has a prime location right above Caleta beach. Not a very private or quiet resort, it has a lively atmosphere, with plenty of activities, games, and music. Simple and clean rooms have terraces. Children under 4 stay free, children 4–12 get 50% off. 255 rooms. Major credit cards.

Hotel Misión $$ *Felipe Valle 12; Tel. (7) 482-3643; fax (7) 482-2076.* This 19th-century building offers simply furnished rooms with colonial touches, surrounding a central courtyard. All rooms have ceiling fans and private baths with showers (no A/C). A traditional Pozole dinner is served every Thursday afternoon. Located in walking distance from the zócolo. 28 rooms. No credit cards.

Westin Las Brisas $$$$$ *Carretera Escénica 5255, Las Brisas; Tel. (7)469-6900; fax (7) 446-5328.* This resort, with its pink and white villas, made Acapulco famous—synonymous with romance and jet-set-style fun. The resort is located on a hill, with access to its exclusive beach across the highway. There's a US$20 daily service charge, and daily continental breakfast is included. Wheelchair access. 263 rooms. Major credit cards.

Villa Vera Hotel Spa & Racquet Club $$$$ *Lomas del Mar 35; Fracc. Club Deportivo; Tel (7)484-0333; fax (7) 484-7479.* This star-quality boutique hotel has recently been returned to its former splendor. Each suite has been tastefully and individually decorated. Romantic and pampering, it offers a super location high on a hill, three blocks away from La Condesa beach. No children under 16 allowed. Beautiful gardens, 6 pools, 4 tennis courts, and a complete spa. 68 rooms. Major credit cards.

Zihuatanejo

Villas San Sebastián $$$$ *Boulevard Escénico Playa La Ropa; Tel. (7) 554-2084; fax (7) 554-3220.* Beautiful suites with air-conditioned bedrooms and open air living areas that include equipped kitchenettes. Built on the hillside, two blocks away from the beach, with views to Playa La Ropa. The newer units have intriguing architectural details and superior ocean views. All rooms are tastefully decorated in pale tropical colors. 9 rooms. No credit cards. Major credit cards.

Villa del Sol $$$$$ *Playa La Ropa; Tel. (7) 554-2239; fax (7) 5542758-44066.* With exquisitely designed split-level suites on the best beach in Zihua, this resort has a reputation for high-priced exclusivity, bordering on the pretentious. Rooms are sophisticated, with exceptional attention to detail. Children are accepted from mid-April to mid-November. Two restaurants serve haute-cuisine —part of the overall experience, as a $60US daily meal plan purchase is required. 55 rooms. Major credit cards.

Villas Miramar $$$ *Adelita 78, Playa Madera; Tel. (7) 554-2106; fax (7) 554-2149.* An attractive hotel surrounded by gardens, with an atmosphere reminiscent of a traditional Mexican home. Rooms are very clean and basic, with two double beds and private bathrooms with showers. There are two pools, and a restaurant open for breakfast and lunch only. 18 rooms. Major credit cards.

Ixtapa

Krystal $$$$ *Boulevard Ixtapa s/n; Tel. (7) 553 0333; fax (7) 553 0216.* One of the most welcoming large resorts in all of Mexico, this hotel has maintained a large percentage of its original staff. Nicely appointed rooms are spacious and bright, with great ocean and garden views. Beautifully kept grounds surround a large pool. The beach is nice for sunning, but not safe for swimming. Wheelchair access. 255 rooms. Major credit cards.

Westin Brisas Ixtapa $$$$$ *Playa Vistahermosa s/n; Tel. (7) 553-2121; fax (7) 553-1091.* A most stunning resort set on top of a cliff; every room has a spectacular view. Excellent service and a welcoming attitude truly reflects the *"Mi casa es su casa"* philosophy. Simple, rather small rooms have terraces and all the necessary comforts for a truly civilized stay. Five restaurants, pool by the beach. Wheelchair access. 423 rooms. Major credit cards.

Huatulco

Quinta Real $$$$$ *Boulevard Benito Juárez Lote 2, Bahía de Tangolunda; Tel. (9) 581 0428; fax (9) 581 0429.* This is an elegant resort that caters mostly to honeymooners or those looking for romance. Rooms are on stepped levels, overlooking the bay below. Luxurious comforts include terraces with hammocks and marble Jacuzzi tubs. Suites have large living areas. The restaurant is one of the best in Huatulco. 27 units. Major credit cards.

Misión de los Arcos $$ *Gardenia 902, La Crucecita; Tel. (9) 587 0165; fax (9) 587 1135.* A more economical version of the Quinta Real style, with a great location one block from the plaza in Crucecita. Offers nicely appointed, light and airy rooms, some with air-conditioning. Gym and beach club accessible by a free shuttle, twice a day. Scheduled to add restaurant and pool. 13 rooms. Major credit cards.

Hotel Meigas Binniguenda $$$ *Boulevard Santa Cruz 201, Bahía de Santa Cruz de Huatulco; Tel. (9) 587 0077; fax*

(9) 587 0284. An all-inclusive resort with a Mexican atmosphere to it. Rooms are decorated in Mexican colonial style, all have air conditioning, TV, and ample tiled baths with showers. Nice pool. Beach club with free shuttle every hour. 165 rooms. Major credit cards.

Puerto Escondido

Hotel Santa Fé $$ *Calle del Morro s/n, Col. Marinero; Tel. (9) 582 0170; fax (9) 582 0260.* An excellent value with discounts of 30% in May, June, September, and October. Rooms are spread among hacienda-style structures, surrounding a courtyard with two swimming pools and tropical gardens. Excellent service from the attentive staff makes the stay even more pleasant! Ample rooms are decorated with Mexican colonial accents, and the town's best restaurant is on-site. Wheelchair access. 69 rooms. Major credit cards.

Hotel Paraíso Escondido $$ *Calle Unión 10 Col Centro; Tel. (9) 582 0444; 20 rooms.* Built in a rambling hacienda-style house, this eclectic inn offers small details that delight the passerby at every step, and sweeping views of the bay. All rooms are decorated with beautiful Mexican antiques. A sculpture garden surrounds a pool and wading pool. Located a couple of blocks from the beach. Wheelchair access. No credit cards.

Hotel Arco Iris $ *Calle del Morro s/n, Playa Zicatela; Tel. (9) 582 0432; fax (9) 582 1494.* Built in a large three story Mexican-style house on the beach, the simply appointed rooms have large private balconies or terraces, mosquito net draped beds, Oaxacan bedspreads, and amazing views. Some rooms have kitchenettes, but there is no air conditioning. The top-floor restaurant/bar is a local favorite for happy hours. 26 rooms. MC, V.

Recommended Restaurants

Dining along Mexico's Pacific coast is generally a casual affair, with some of the best meals served in rustic palapa-topped restaurants at the ocean's edge. Even the finest restaurants prefer their patrons be comfortable and enjoy the main event—the exquisite seasonings and subtle distinction in flavors when seafood, vegetables, and fruits are supplied from local sources.

Most hotel restaurants are fine for any meal, with their ample breakfast buffets a favored indulgence. However if you really want to sample the tastes and smells of Mexico you should venture out and dine at locally owned cafes and restaurants—just be willing to try new dishes and you may find you've had a truly outstanding culinary experience. Mexico is especially renown for its many inexpensive options, from the ubiquitous taco stands, to the welcoming small *fondas* that serve set menus for breakfast and lunch at rock-bottom prices. As a rule, small restaurants accept only cash for payment; the more tourist-oriented places are more likely to accept US dollars. However, it's generally is a good idea to have pesos at hand when you dine out.

The following listed prices are for a three-course meal, excluding drinks and tips. More expensive menu items—such as shrimp or lobster—will increase these average checks.

Note that the busiest times in Mexican restaurants are between 2 and 3pm for lunch service, and between 9pm and 11pm for dinner. During high season, reservations may be needed at fine dining restaurants.

$$$$	over US$25
$$$	US$15–US$25
$$	US$5–US$15
$	less than US$$5

Puerto Vallarta

Archie's Wok $$$ *Francisca Rodríguez 130; Tel. (3) 222 0411.* Open Monday–Saturday 2pm–11pm; closed September. Exquisite Thai and Asian food, with a specialty of fish and seafood—fresh, spicy and tasty—served in a serene garden setting. The *lumpias* (eggrolls) and fried Thai noodles are excellent. Great bar drinks both alcoholic and non-alcoholic—try the Thai Mai Tai. Live flute and guitar music Wednesday–Saturday. Major credit cards.

Café Maximilian $$$$ *Olas Altas 380-B; Tel. (3) 223 0760.* Open Monday–Saturday 6pm–11pm. An Austrian style-restaurant with fine food served in an elegant, yet casual *bistro* setting, with sidewalk dining available. Sautéed squid and San Blas shrimp are tasty starters; and the delicate trout almondine is divine. Classic European-style pork and veal dishes are also specialties. Major credit cards.

Fonda El Patio $ *Francia 139; No phone.* Open Monday–Saturday 1pm–5pm. A traditional *fonda* where many locals enjoy lunch. Homemade food is served by the prompt and friendly staff. You can choose from the set menu or have a grilled steak or chicken breast with a couple of homemade *quesadillas*. The tortillas are handmade and the beans are always done to perfection. No credit cards.

La Palapa $$–$$$ *Púlpito 103; Tel. (3) 222 5225.* Open daily 8am–11pm. A Vallarta classic since 1959, locals frequent this seaside restaurant for their wonderful breakfasts and casual lunches that may include use of a beach chair and shade palapa on Vallarta's most popular beach. When the sun sets, the restaurant takes on a more formal tone, with elegant seafood specialties and exquisite deserts. Live music nightly. Major credit cards.

The Red Cabbage/El Repollo Rojo $$ *Calle Rivera del Río 204-A; Tel (3) 223 0411*. Open daily 5pm–11pm. A small, funky restaurant located away from the main tourist area, this is a showcase of national cultural icons, dominated by images of Frida Kahlo. Specialties include true Mexican classics, including an outstanding *sopa de frijol* and worthy *chiles en nogada*. The food is well seasoned and cooked. No credit cards.

Trío Café–Restaurant–Bar $$$$ *Guerrero 264; Tel. (3) 222 219*. Open daily 6pm–midnight. Lunch Monday–Friday, noon–4pm high season only. Widely considered the best restaurant in Vallarta, Trio has exquisite, unpretentious food, attentive service, a welcoming atmosphere, and charming hosts. European-born chefs-owner Bernard Güth and Peter Lodes are true geniuses that love to explore the endless possibilities of combining Mediterranean cuisine with the regional ingredients of the Mexican coast. Highly recommended. Major credit cards.

Manzanillo

Willy's $$$ *Crucero de Las Brisas; (3) 333 1794*. Open daily 7pm–midnight. Casual, and always crowded, Willy's is a Manzanillo institution, located on the beachfront of the Las Brisas section. Grilled fresh fish and lobster, as well as steaks and duck, are specialties on a menu where almost everything is a delight. The atmosphere is comfortable, and there's live music on weekends. MC, V.

Zihuatanejo

Kau-Kan $$$$$ *Camino a Playa la Ropa s/n; Tel. (7) 554 8446*. Open daily 1:30pm–10:30pm. One of the few places where you have to dress for dinner. The atmosphere is casually refined in this open-air, stucco-walled restaurant that offers an expansive view of the bay. The freshest ingredients are used to prepare the daily specials, which always include fish and seafood cooked in innovative preparations. Major credit cards.

Nueva Zelanda $$ *Cuauhtemoc 23 and Ejido; Tel. (7) 554-2340.* Open daily 8am–10pm. One of the most popular places in town, frequented by locals and tourists alike, the food here is prepared fresh under the owner's watchful eye. Superb breakfasts and delicious cappucinos. Liquados, tortas, and enchiladas are some of the traditional menu favorites. No credit cards.

Ruben's $$ *Calle Adelita s/n; (7) 554 4617.* Open daily 6pm–11pm. Long-time residents and loyal return customers attest to the fact that these are the best grilled burgers on the Mexican Pacific and other coasts. Accompanied by tasty grilled vegetables that include chayote, zucchini, and corn. Simple, easy—not fast—but extremely good food. No credit cards.

Ixtapa

Beccofino $$$$ *Marina Ixtapa; Tel. (7) 553 1770.* Open daily 9am–12midnight. A long-standing tradition for refined and lively dining in the Marina, this place is usually crowded with locals and return customers enjoying Beccofino's original northern Italian recipes. The ravioli are superb. Major credit cards.

Restaurant El Faro de Pacifica $$$–$$$$ *Paseo de la Colina s/n, Col. Vista Hermosa; Tel. (7) 5531027, ext 815.* Open daily 8am–11:30pm. This restaurant offers a spectacular view of Ixtapa. While it is usually empty for breakfast and lunch, it reigns elegantly at night, when it draws the largest crowd. If nothing else it is worth a visit to enjoy the view. Dinner specialties emphasize fish and seafood with a Nouvelle Mexican twist. Major credit cards.

Acapulco

Casa Nova $$$$ *Carretera Escénica 5256; Tel. (7) 484 6819.* Open daily 7pm–11 pm. Overlooking the bay, this Italian restaurant exudes class and taste to match the view. The food is divine and the service unrivaled in Acapulco. Romantic atmosphere. Reservations required. Major credit cards.

El Amigo Miguel $$ *Juárez 16; Tel. (7) 483 6981.* Open daily 10am–10 pm. Some of the best fresh seafood at the best prices. Frequented by locals and Mexican tourists looking to indulge in the delicacies of the sea. Anything *al mojo de ajo* is finger-lickin-good. Simple decoration lets you focus on the meal. The music is loud and the place is always busy. An authentic Mexican seafood restaurant. Major credit cards.

El Cabrito $$ *Costera Miguel Alemán 1480; Tel. (7) 484 7711.* Monday–Saturday 2pm–1am, Sunday 2pm–11pm. A long-time favorite for this authentic specialty of northern Mexico, *cabrito* —roasted kid. You'll also find *machaca* (shredded dried beef) cooked in a zesty sauce, tasty mole, and other specialties from around the country. Major credit cards.

La Petite Belgique $$$ *Plaza Marbella (across from La Diana); Tel (7) 484 7725.* Open daily 2pm–midnight. Low season closed on Tuesday. An exceptional little restaurant that has been a well kept secret for locals. Perhaps one of the best refined yet casual seafood and European-style restaurants in all of the

Pacific coast, with personal attention provided by the charming owner. The mussels are positively divine, flown in fresh daily. Major credit cards.

Spicey $$$$ *Carretera Escénica s/n; Tel. (7) 446 6003.* Open daily 7pm–11:30pm. A sleek, hip place to dine and enjoy the trendy upscale atmosphere, with sweeping views across Acapulco Bay. Their interesting menu features intriguing flavor combinations for fresh seafood and fish. Beautiful and mouthwatering. Major credit cards.

Su Casa $$$$ *Ave. Anahuac 110; Tel. (7) 484 4350.* Open daily 6pm–midnight. This open-air restaurant sits on a hillside, with spectacular views of the city. A constantly changing menu, supervised by the owners, guarantees the quality of the food. Seafood, fish, and Mexican specialties are always available. Reservations recommended. MC, V.

Huatulco

El Sabor de Oaxaca $–$$ *Ave. Guamuchil 206, Crucecita; Tel. (9) 587 0060.* Open daily 7am–midnight. Plain but pleasant atmosphere to enjoy authentic Oaxacan food. *Mole negro* is the big winner when it comes to Oaxacan food—a delicate sauce made with 22 different spices. Or arrive hungry and try their ample sampler plate. Also great for breakfast. Major credit cards.

Il Giardino de Papa $$$ *Flamboyán 204, Crucecita; Tel. (9) 587 1763.* Open daily 3pm–11pm; closed Tuesday in low season. Who could pass up a meal prepared by the same chef who cooked for the Pope? If nothing else, finding out what Mario, the chef, is now doing in Huatulco is worth a visit to this casually elegant garden restaurant. Furthermore, the fresh-made pastas are always done to perfection. Major credit cards.

Tipsy's $–$$ *Bahía Santa Cruz (next to Escollera); Tel. (9) 587 0576.* Open daily 9am–7pm. This casual beach club and water-ski school has one of the better restaurants along this strip. The food is a little heavier than in most beach restaurants, with lots of beef in the menu, but there are also seafood and fresh fish options. The bar stays open until 11pm. No credit cards.

Puerto Escondido

Carmen's La Patisserie/El Cafecito $–$$ *Playa Marinero/Calle del Morro s/n, Playa Zicatela; No phone..* Open Monday–Saturday 7am–3pm, Sunday 7am–noon, Wednesday–Monday 6am–10pm; closed for dinner Tuesday. There are no words to adequately describe Carmen's pastries, especially the mango éclairs, accompanied by heavenly espresso drinks served iced or hot. Lunch specials include fresh fruit shakes, delicious sandwiches, and spinach-stuffed puff pastries. Shrimp dinners at El Cafecito go for fewer than 50 pesos (US$6). Morning to midnight, this sidewalk café is deservedly packed. No credit cards.

Restaurante Santa Fé $$$ *Calle del Morro s/n (in Hotel Hotel Santa Fé); Tel. (9) 582 0170.* Open daily 7am–11pm. Vegetarian, seafood, and Mexican cuisine, served in a relaxed atmosphere across from Zicatela beach. Fresh tuna, when in season, has never been better prepared. An exceptional restaurant and outstanding value, a refined respite in this otherwise casual resort. Attentive service, full bar, and occasional live music. Major credit cards.

INDEX